TOP OF THE CLASS

TOP OF THE CLASS

How Asian Parents Raise High Achievers— and How You Can Too

DR. SOO KIM ABBOUD
and JANE KIM

BERKLEY BOOKS, NEW YORK

THE BERKLEY PUBLISHING GROUP
Published by the Penguin Group
Penguin Group (USA) Inc.
375 Hudson Street, New York, New York 10014, USA
Penguin Group (Canada), 90 Eglinton Avenue East, Suite 700, Toronto, Ontario M4P 2Y3, Canada
(a division of Pearson Penguin Canada Inc.)
Penguin Books Ltd., 80 Strand, London WC2R 0RL, England
Penguin Group Ireland, 25 St. Stephen's Green, Dublin 2, Ireland (a division of Penguin Books Ltd.)
Penguin Group (Australia), 250 Camberwell Road, Camberwell, Victoria 3124, Australia
(a division of Pearson Australia Group Pty. Ltd.)
Penguin Books India Pvt. Ltd., 11 Community Centre, Panchsheel Park, New Delhi—110 017, India
Penguin Group (NZ), Cnr. Airborne and Rosedale Roads, Albany, Auckland 1310, New Zealand
(a division of Pearson New Zealand Ltd.)
Penguin Books (South Africa) (Pty.) Ltd., 24 Sturdee Avenue, Rosebank, Johannesburg 2196,
South Africa

Penguin Books Ltd., Registered Offices: 80 Strand, London WC2R 0RL, England

This book is an original publication of The Berkley Publishing Group.

Cover design by Pyrographix.
Text design by Tiffany Estreicher.

—

PRINTING HISTORY
Berkley trade paperback edition / November 2005

Berkley trade paperback ISBN: 0-425-20561-4

This book has been catalogued with the Library of Congress

PRINTED IN THE UNITED STATES OF AMERICA

10 9 8 7 6 5 4 3 2

This book is dedicated to our parents,
Jae and Dae Kim. Thank you for everything.

Acknowledgments

Soo would like to thank her husband, Joe, whose passion for life and learning is unparalleled. Many years after leaving home, Soo still finds it hard to believe that she married someone whose love and commitment to lifelong learning even surpasses her parents' and her own.

The authors would also like to collectively thank a few people. Thanks go out to our wonderful literary agent, Wendy Sherman, who championed this project from merely a concept to the book you are reading today. Many thanks to Denise Silvestro and Katie Day for their wonderful editorial advice and support. We would also like to thank all of our educators, our friends whose stories we revealed throughout our book, as well as the prominent Asian-Americans who took the time to contribute thoughtful quotes. This book would not have been possible without your help.

Contents

Foreword

Have you ever sat next to an Asian student in class and wondered how she managed to consistently get straight A's while you struggled to maintain a B-minus average? Or wondered why the percentage of Asian students enrolled at the top colleges is disproportionately high? Asian students are considered amongst the best and the brightest in America. And although we hesitate to stereotype all Asian students, we cannot deny that, as a whole, they are doing something right.

If you don't believe us, just check out the following statistics. While Asian-Americans make up only 4% of the U.S. population, Asian-American students make up a much higher percentage of students in top universities around the country. Among Ivy League schools, the percentages are astounding: 23% at the University of Pennsylvania, 25% at Columbia and Cornell, 15% at Brown, and 18% at Harvard. Asian-Americans make up 24% of the student population at Stanford, 15% at Johns Hopkins, 17% at Northwestern, and a whopping 42% at the University of California at Berkeley (despite making up only 11% of the population in California).

In addition, 47% of Asian and Pacific Islanders over the age of twenty-five hold a Bachelor's degree or higher, while the corresponding rate for all adults in this age group is much lower, 27%. Sixteen percent of Asians and Pacific Islanders over the age of twenty-five hold an advanced degree (i.e., master's, PhD, MD, or JD), in contrast to 9% for all other adults in this age group. A startling 15% of all U.S. physicians and surgeons are of Asian descent (statistics made available from the U.S. Census Bureau). And the buck doesn't stop there. After outperforming their colleagues in school, Asian-Americans also bring home higher incomes than their non-Asian counterparts; in 2002, the median income for Asian and Pacific Islanders was $52,018, almost $10,000 higher than the median household income for the rest of the population ($42,409).

So what do these numbers signify? Certainly Asian-Americans are no more intelligent than any other race or ethnic group. Contrary to what the public may believe, Asian students are no more intellectually gifted than non-Asian students. *The reason that Asian students outperform their peers in the classroom has nothing to do with how they are born and everything to do with how they are raised. This book is for all parents and children who want to discover (or rediscover) a love for learning and develop the discipline to use this love to build knowledge and indispensable skills in the classroom and beyond.*

You may be asking—who are we to write this book, and why are we writing it? Well, we're happy to tell you. Soo is a board-certified surgeon and an assistant professor at the University of Pennsylvania; Jane is an attorney and immigration specialist at The Children's Hospital of Philadelphia. We are first-generation Korean-Americans—that is to say, our parents, Jae and Dae Kim, were born in Korea but emigrated to the United States prior to having us.

Our parents came to America with their heads full of dreams of a better life but with little money in their pockets. Although they had stars in their eyes, their early life in America was far from glamorous. After moving into a small one-bedroom apartment on the University of Southern California's campus (where our father was getting his master's degree in Computer Science), our mother went to work as a seamstress. She worked twelve- to fourteen-hour days for less than minimum wage with a dozen other immigrant women who were trying to help their husbands and families financially. Our father worked evenings as a janitor and as a gas-station attendant to make ends meet. He barely had time to study but somehow managed to obtain his degree after two years.

Soo was born two years after our parents came to America, Jane three years later. Our parents traveled from California to Toronto, Canada, and finally to Raleigh, North Carolina, as our father climbed the ranks of Nortel Networks (formerly Northern Telecom). Our mother stopped working outside the home after she had us and concentrated her efforts on educating her children. Our parents were never able to provide us with designer clothing or trips to the Caribbean, but we were never lacking for love or attention. Not once during our childhood did we ever doubt that our happiness, education, and future were our parents' top priorities.

Soo was the typical smart, quiet Asian kid throughout grade school and high school. She got straight A's and won math competitions instead of sports trophies. She attended math camp in the summer instead of partying at the beach with friends. Jane was a bit more social and outgoing. Nevertheless, her main goal in school was to get good grades rather than be seen wearing the latest fashion. Sound boring or even painful? Not at all. We are now successful career women who are fulfilled both professionally and personally. We have wonderful relationships with our parents (and each other!) and have only the fondest memories of our childhood.

Growing up, we noticed that many of our fellow Asian-Americans had similar experiences and views on education and professional development. Like ours, their parents had made education one of their children's top priorities.

Needless to say, we are proud of what we and other Asian-Americans have accomplished. More importantly, however, we are convinced that ingredients specific to an Asian upbringing best prepare a child for success in the classroom and beyond. In this book, our hope is to share these secrets with you.

If you are wondering whether we were always at the top of our class, the answer is no. Soo struggled with advanced science courses and Jane experienced more than her fair share of mediocre grades throughout college and law school. But we made our way through and are now two financially secure professionals. Like many Asian immigrants, our parents came to Los Angeles with little money in their pockets and dreams of a better life. Thirty years later, we still smile when we hear our parents brag to friends and family, "One doctor and one lawyer in the family—who could ask for anything more?" Although this book will not guarantee that your child will be an exceptional student or college valedictorian, what it *will* do is help bring out the best student in your child by nurturing a lifelong love of learning and a true commitment to education.

Of course, professional success does not guarantee personal fulfillment and happiness, but it certainly helps. This book can show you how to maximize your chances of raising children who are successful at school and in the workplace by adopting the principles of many Asian immigrant parents. Each child is unique, as is each family; however, if some of our secrets make their way into your child's life, we guarantee your child will be a better student for it.

Secret 1

Instill a Love and Need for Learning and Education

The most important thing parents can give to their children is love—but a desire and love for learning and education comes in as a close second. Many parents find it difficult to instill this passion for learning in their kids. Not surprisingly, years later these parents find themselves wondering why their son or daughter has no interest in going to college, much less to graduate school. It's never too early to start encouraging a love of learning in your child. In fact, early childhood is the best time to start, as young minds have an incredible capacity to absorb information and establish the necessary values that set the stage for future success.

But before we begin discussing how to get your child to love learning, let us first explain the major reason parents today find it difficult to pass this love on: very few adults today actually love to learn. We live in a society that seeks comfort and leisure above all else; the "American dream" typically includes a home complete with a big-screen TV and state-of-the-art grill. Many working parents today punch in and punch out, in a hurry to get home to sit in front of the TV. They view the process of learning and education as part of their thankfully distant past—for the majority of us Americans, learning and education stopped after high school and college. After all, hitting the books for more than a decade is enough for any lifetime, isn't it?

Learning should be a lifelong process, not something that stops abruptly in one's early twenties. When your kids are young and start going to school, you as parents are their main role models. They equate the way you approach your job with the way they should approach their jobs (school). If you have to drag yourself out of bed every morning and complain about how miserable your job is as you drop your child off at school, chances are he or she will do the same.

If you're finding this concept difficult to swallow, think hard about your friends and family. How many of them do you truly believe love to learn new things, love the field they are in, or look for new ways in which to grow? On the other hand, how often have you heard parents gripe about their job or vocation?

We would venture to say quite often (and we would be guilty as well). Perhaps you can even relate to what we are saying. Parents have only the best intentions when it comes to raising their children, and all want to be ideal role models in the home. However, it is hard not to complain about a boring or stagnant job or a rough day when you finally return to the comforts of your own home and family. Even if you enjoy your job or career, you might need someone to vent to after an especially tough day. Who better to express your frustrations than to your spouse and kids, right?

We disagree.

Children have no more powerful role models than their parents. Children who witness their parents in an abusive relationship will often learn to abuse others or become victims. On the other hand, children whose parents value family will likely learn to do the same. It's amazing that so few parents realize how powerful an influence they are in their children's lives, and how certain behaviors can negatively impact their beloved offspring.

Along the same lines, if your child sees that you appreciate and love learning, he or she will learn to do the same. If your child sees that you look forward to going to work every morning, he or she will view work (and school) as rewarding and fun. If your child sees that you dread your job, call in sick every chance you get, or badmouth your work environment or colleagues, he or she will come to believe that schooling and education will only bring misery in the future.

You are your child's best role model, so be enthusiastic toward learning and education—and your career.

It is important to know that an education alone does not ensure happiness or professional success. We know many unhappy people with advanced degrees and hefty paychecks. However, a love for continued learning and advancement in any occupation is essential to professional happiness. Without making this love evident in your life, there is little chance your child will think of any profession as fulfilling.

Right about now, you might be thinking that it's possible to love learning but hate your job. You might love going to museums in your time off and learning about architecture or archeology but hate your job as a data processor or store manager. While this is certainly possible for many Americans, we still firmly stand by our belief that a love for learning and commitment to advancement can make any job, however dull or stagnant, substantially better. Perhaps you hate your job punching in numbers all day and all you can think of is that managerial position in your company that seems so out of reach. If all you do is punch in and do the least amount of data entry possible for that day to avoid criticism from your boss, chances are you'll never be fulfilled enough to excel at your job and get that promotion. On the other hand, if you take advanced typing or data-entry courses to exceed your quota and distinguish yourself amongst your peers as a high producer, and then discuss with your boss taking managerial courses to increase your chances of a promotion, it's likely your job happiness will substantially increase.

Always create ways to actively include learning in your profession. This will dramatically increase your career advancement opportunities and add to your sense of professional fulfillment in a way that will benefit both you and your child.

Of course, no job is perfect, and everyone is entitled to a bad day. If you hate your job and want to complain about it, do so to your spouse or friends, and bite your tongue around your children. Even go as far as to act excited about your career. If you absolutely cannot (we know it's hard sometimes), at least take up activities or hobbies that you are excited about and share this passion with your children.

For those parents who are extremely disappointed with their careers and want to ensure that their children experience the excitement and pride an intellectually stimulating job provides, make it a point to surround your children on a regular basis with adults who are clearly empowered and enlightened by their professions. Surrounding yourselves and your children with these adult role models will not only whet your child's appetite for learning, but it may even inspire you.

A close friend of Soo's from middle school was a first generation

Chinese-American named Angela. Her parents were hard-working immigrants who had opened a nail salon in the suburbs of Raleigh, North Carolina, where the rent was cheap and the public schools reputable. Angela's parents worked twelve-hour days, breathing in noxious fumes from the polish and alcohol all day long. After several years of extremely hard work, they had amassed enough money to employ all of their siblings, who moved to the United States one by one. Despite their financial success, Angela's parents had become increasingly disgruntled with their profession. Some days, Angela's mother could barely drag herself out of bed to go to work.

As you might expect, Angela was quite aware of how unhappy her parents were in the business, and it caused her much distress. Every day after school she would rush to the nail salon to relieve her mother of her duties. As a result, her grades began to suffer. Although she became a top-notch manicurist, she was miserable. She nearly failed out of seventh grade, a difficult feat for someone as bright as she was.

Angela had two big problems. First, her parents had allowed their daughter to assume responsibility for their unhappiness. In other words, Angela had taken it upon herself to "save" her parents by rushing home from school and helping out at the salon. Angela's parents wanted their daughter to make school her top priority, but by allowing her to work at the salon rather than concentrate on schoolwork, they failed to make that desire clear. Second, Angela's parents regularly complained about their jobs in her presence, to the point that she began viewing work as an undesirable yet unavoidable aspect of everyday life. As a seventh-grader, Angela's "job" was to keep up with her assignments and do well in school. However, having adopted a similar attitude as her parents toward her "day job," Angela's grades began to fall.

Angela's failure at school initially came as a shock to her parents, who did not realize how negatively their daughter's schoolwork was being affected. Upon discovering that their child's grades had suffered, Angela's parents resolved to change their habits. They stopped complaining about work, and they immediately hired help (despite wanting to keep profits in the family) so that Angela could concentrate on schoolwork and so that her mother could relax and spend some quality time with her daughter.

Angela's mother relished her time off. Now with more free time than she had known in several years, Mrs. Tan became active in the Parent-Teacher Association (PTA) and in the community. Despite her shyness and broken English, she befriended many of the parents at our small middle school. She offered free manicure services (who doesn't love a nice manicure?) to many of the PTA women, who got to know her on a more intimate level; soon, they began inviting her and Mr. Tan to dinner parties and community events. Slowly but surely, Mrs. Tan also began to view her work as a way to bring the community together, and this greatly added to her professional fulfillment.

In addition to becoming a better role model for her daughter, Mrs. Tan was now in good company with architects, physicians, businessmen, lawyers, and computer programmers, many of whom loved what they did for a living and were eager to share their passion with the younger generation. Although Mrs. Tan realized she might not ever be the ideal model of professional fulfillment or joyous lifelong learning for her daughter, she now had many newfound friends who were. Eager to get her daughter excited about learning, Mrs. Tan soon began asking her friends if they would sit down with Angela and share with her what had led them to their respected professions. Soon Angela found herself having lengthy discussions with these men and women, all of whom delighted in sharing how they beat the odds to secure professions that fulfilled them intellectually and personally. Angela specifically recalls speaking with a software designer whose creativity and technological ingenuity left an indelible impression. After spending a few days at his office and taking computer-programming classes in the summers, her mind was made up. Angela eventually graduated from the University of California at San Diego and became the vice president of a start-up company in Silicon Valley during the Clinton years, the golden era of technology. Today, Angela's family is doing extremely well. Her mother continues to work at the salon part-time and now relishes her role in bringing the women in the community together for regular 'manicure parties' to discuss parenting, opportunities for professional advancement, and social events.

Surround your children with people who love learning and are in diverse fields. This will allow your children to develop a healthy respect for learning while also giving them information to pursue various career paths.

If community events and PTA meetings are not your cup of tea, there are other ways you can instill a love of learning and education in your child. Allow us to share another success story with a different slant. Janet was the eldest daughter of our church's minister, Reverend Suh. Reverend and Mrs. Suh were deeply religious and loved their roles as leaders of the church community. Although they attempted to share their passion for God's work and study of the Gospel with their fourteen-year-old daughter, like many children of religious professionals, she rebelled. She wanted no part of the church and could barely be forced to get out of bed for the eleven o'clock Sunday service, let alone attend the teen Bible study group on Wednesday evenings.

Although disheartened that Janet would not follow in his footsteps, Reverend Suh wanted to make sure that his daughter learned the value of education and experienced the thrill of learning firsthand. Janet was a bright and gifted girl, and her father wanted to provide her with opportunities to learn about different career paths from people who genuinely loved what they did for a living. In essence, he wanted to whet his daughter's appetite for a challenging and intellectually stimulating career—even if it was not in a field of his choice.

A love of learning is imperative to success in any field and should be promoted with enthusiasm despite any objections you might have toward the professions your child wishes to pursue.

That's when he came up with the idea of having a "Career Day." At the time, our church's congregation consisted of several hundred Korean-Americans, many of whom had recently emigrated to the United States. There was a plethora of PhDs, pharmacists, physicians, business executives, accountants, and engineers in the congregation. With the help of his congregation, Reverend Suh began announcing and advertising a monthly Career Day at the end of his services. Each month, a member of the church would meet with the youth group (children from elementary to high school) to talk about his or her profession and share reasons for pursuing it. A Q&A session would follow.

At first, Janet resisted the idea of having to stay at church even longer than usual. Career Day typically took place after Sunday service and lunch. Suddenly, Sundays turned from tolerable one-hour affairs into dreaded half-day affairs. Nevertheless, she was forced to attend, as were we.

Initially, Janet would sit in the back corner of the room, smacking her gum loudly and fidgeting in her chair. This created such a distraction that some of the more attentive children could barely concentrate on what the speaker was saying. As various speakers took center stage, Janet continued her gum-smacking and rude comments, saying things like, "God, I need to get out of here and smoke a cigarette!" Several Sundays passed, with no change in her behavior. But one Sunday, everything changed.

She was absolutely stunning, which immediately put the boys in the group on their best behavior. Her name was Myung Park, and she was a pharmacist at a local university hospital. Her eyes lit up as she spoke of her profession and the satisfaction she obtained from aiding patients with medications, as well as ensuring their safety. She could not have spoken for more than two minutes before we heard Janet cursing under her breath about how any idiot could dispense drugs off of pharmacy shelves. "It's not like you're a doctor or anything," Janet added with a smirk, obviously hoping her nasty comments would put an end to the session. Boy, was she wrong.

Myung's beautiful almond eyes immediately focused on the rowdy teenager and narrowed with displeasure. In a soft but no-nonsense tone, she quickly put the pastor's daughter in her place, a feat no member of the church (including her parents) had been able to do. "Comments like that show just how misguided you are," she said pointedly. "Too bad your insecurity makes you look down on people who are happy with their work. When you get older, your attitude will stop you from reaching your full potential. When you're ready to talk like an adult, my door will be open. In the meantime, shut up so that others can listen."

The audience gasped as all eyes turned to Janet, anticipating her rebuttal or noisy departure. There was none—a beet-red Janet remained quietly in her seat while the rest of us (mostly the guys) talked with Myung about the pharmaceutical industry.

Janet never did attend another Career Day, but Myung had left an indelible impression on her. During the next few years, Janet frequently visited Myung at work and eventually became a pharmacist herself. Last we heard, Janet was working in the field of pharmaceutical development.

The message is clear. The best way to get your children excited about lifelong learning and higher education is to surround them with people who are excited about learning and their careers.

The second reason parents have difficulty guiding their children to love learning and education is that many parents are hard-pressed for time. It takes time to instill a love of learning—precious time that most of us don't have. Many American families today revolve around two working parents or a single parent. After a long day on the job, parents seldom have the energy to spend time teaching their children to read, learn a new word, or practice their arithmetic. Watching TV or playing with your children seems a much more enjoyable and relaxing alternative for your weary minds and bodies. We understand that. Nevertheless, our goal is to inspire you to embrace activities that are educationally rewarding for your child with the same enthusiasm you would approach other pastimes.

> **In order to instill a love for learning and education in your children, you must 1) exhibit this love yourselves or expose your children to people who do portray this love, and 2) joyfully invest the time to teach this love to your children.**

Thinking back to our childhood, we have many wonderful memories of family vacations, Christmas dinners, and trips to the movies. But we also have countless memories of times spent with our parents tackling math problems or deciphering a difficult text. Sound boring? It doesn't have to be, and it certainly wasn't for us.

A wonderful example comes to mind. When Soo was a sophomore in high school, she had to take the PSATs, otherwise known as the pre-SATs. This examination was generally considered a good indicator of how one would do on the SATs, so Soo wanted to score as well as she could. When Soo got her results back, however, she was disappointed. Although she did extremely well on the math portion, her verbal score was nothing to write home about. It seemed that her vocabulary needed improvement.

That surprised her a little at first. Soo had won numerous spelling championships over the years and had always managed to get A's in English. But she had to face the facts—the score didn't lie. She would need to improve her vocabulary and reading-comprehension skills.

Soo was not the only one who was disappointed, of course. After getting over his initial disappointment, our father praised Soo on her math score and asked her how she thought she might improve her verbal score. Soo was at a loss for ideas, with the exception of tackling the entire English dictionary word by word. Thankfully, our father had a better idea.

Days after Soo received her test results, our father scrutinized her suggested summer reading list and selected *Jane Eyre* by Charlotte Bronte. At the time, Soo was an avid reader who had read many classic works beyond her years. However, so as not to interfere with her reading pleasure, she had repeatedly chosen to ignore the words she did not understand. *Jane Eyre* would be the first book that would take her an entire summer to read.

Soo was to read twenty pages a day, which seemed an easy assignment. It was not: she was to highlight each word she did not understand, look the word up in the dictionary, and write out its definition in a separate notebook. Our father, whose English was not as good as Soo's, would also attempt to learn the words by reviewing them with his daughter at the end of the day.

In the beginning, those twenty pages took hours. On average, there were 5 to 6 words per page that Soo did not understand, which translated to about 100 new words a day. What kept Soo going at the end of each day was the excitement that our father himself showed learning the new words. Each day after work, our father would review the vocabulary list Soo had compiled and valiantly attempt to learn it with her. His evident love of learning was contagious and soon Soo began to look forward to the sessions. Looking back, both Soo and our father found the entire process to be a wonderful bonding experience.

Weeks after she started the project, Soo began to notice that many of the words she had learned earlier in the book were repeated in later chapters. The more she read, the fewer words she had to write down. By the end of the book, she was highlighting only one word per page. The time she spent reading went from several hours to under thirty minutes, and her confidence boomed. By the time Soo finished the book, she had incorporated more than 500 new words into her vocabulary. Not only did she improve her verbal SAT score the next year, she gained a deep sense of pride in her accomplishment. Soo never read a book again without fully comprehending every word in it, no matter how long it took.

Of course, there are many different ways to make learning fun and rewarding, and not all them involve hours reading books in the summer. Let us give you another example, one that involves our mother and Soo at a much younger age.

Like many immigrant parents, our mother chose to stay home with her two kids while our father worked to support his family. Of course, we now realize that being a stay-at-home mom is much tougher than most jobs. In addition to making the home run smoothly, our mother's main goal was to educate her children. Unlike our father's didactic approach, our mother attacked learning with a more playful style.

When Soo was only two years old, our mother taught her the

alphabet, numbers, and colors. She used the typical children's books, but she also used some more innovative techniques. Realizing that a two-year-old's attention span was relatively short, our mother minimized the amount of time spent indoors with books. According to our mother, Soo loved going out with her while she ran errands. She would always point to the various signs on the road with curiosity and delight or get her hands on as many products (mostly candy) that she could at the grocery store.

Our mother began asking Soo to identify letters and numbers on everything from road signs to candy wrappers. Within days, Soo was babbling in the car, reading aloud the letters and numbers that she recognized on road signs. Soo eventually became more interested in reading the letters on the wrappers than she was in eating the candy!

These are only a few examples of the many ways parents can teach their children that learning is essential, fun, and rewarding. Our advice to ambitious and loving parents is this: your children will enjoy learning if you show them that learning and education is fun, rewarding, and *worth your time*. We think it's so worth your time that we're going to give you two other examples from our childhood that show how you might educate your children while creating happy childhood memories.

In Asia, decorative school supplies and accessories are extremely popular among children and young adults. Companies spend millions of dollars designing colorful pens, erasers, notebooks, and numerous other school accessories to be purchased by eager students and their parents. Going to the school-supply store is a fun and memorable affair. Although they lived in America while we were going to school, our parents brought many of their Asian traditions with them. While many of our peers compared returning to school to entering a concentration camp, we never dreaded going back. We particularly enjoyed going with our parents to purchase school supplies prior to starting the new school year.

This was the one shopping trip that did not take place at Kmart. Every year, our parents would take us to a special Korean supermarket (these stores are everywhere now and sell everything from food to gifts to school supplies). There, we would rummage through the piles of colorfully decorated pens, pencils, erasers, and notebooks. Jane loved Hello Kitty merchandise (which is now popular in stores across the United States) and would fill her baskets with Hello Kitty paraphernalia. Being a full two and a half years older, Soo felt she was far too mature for Hello Kitty school supplies. Instead, she filled her book bag with fragrant erasers and pencils with hearts on them. Our parents spared no expense, so we typically bought enough supplies to more than last the entire year.

After the shopping spree, we were always eager to use our new supplies. After carefully arranging and proudly displaying our new items on our desks, we would begin "trying out" our new purchases. Jane would write thank-you letters to our parents; Soo would pen semiautobiographical stories about a girl who one day grew up to become a famous writer. Now that we are adults, we understand how important it was for our parents to convey to us that school was exciting and fun. To this day, Jane has a soft spot for Hello Kitty merchandise and will occasionally buy a pen or two for old times' sake.

Our parents were adept at making even the most frivolous activities educationally rewarding in some way. Even a fun, relaxing family activity like going to the movies was not without an educational slant. We remember our entire family going to the movie *Ghostbusters,* which remains one of our favorite childhood memories. After pigging out on buttery popcorn, candy, and Coke, and laughing so hard our stomachs hurt (we couldn't tell whether it was from laughing or the candy), our family returned home in good spirits. With the movie still fresh in our minds, our parents challenged us to use the experience to broaden our knowledge base. Soo was encouraged to study the periodic table of elements;

Jane learned about Mars by reading our *Encyclopedia Britannica* (our parents told her that the ghosts from *Ghostbusters* were born there).

As you can see, our parents took the time to incorporate learning and education into all of our activities. Indeed, many of our fondest childhood memories involve learning or educational games. We may not have the same memories as many of our peers, but they are happy ones all the same. The most important thing to remember is that learning should not be associated solely with school or "work," but rather with every fun family activity.

Incorporate learning and education into all your children's activities so that they don't associate learning primarily with school or homework.

The third reason that parents find it difficult to instill a love and respect for learning and education is that their actions don't complement their words. In other words, it is easy to *tell* your child that he or she must attend college or get good grades. It is not so easy to alter your lifestyle or make sacrifices in order to give your child the best possible chance at obtaining a top-notch education or receiving a stellar report card. Every chance you get you can say that your child's education and commitment to learning is your top priority. However, if your actions don't support what you are saying, your words will fall on deaf ears. Children are smart—they can easily distinguish between what you say and what you do. On that note, two specific examples come to mind.

A close friend of Jane's was an Indian-American named Susan. Susan's parents were both physicians in busy university-affiliated settings. Both had earned their medical degrees from top institutions and were highly regarded in the medical community. They were also extremely busy and routinely worked twelve- to fourteen-hour days, often leaving Susan in the care of a neighbor or babysitter. When they did spend time with their daughter, they tried to stress the importance of higher education. Pointing to the walls that were covered with their diplomas, they truly believed that their daughter would be motivated to achieve educational greatness simply by being surrounded by it. They were wrong.

According to Susan, her parents derived little pleasure or happiness from their high-powered professions. She recalls anxiously waiting for them to come home, only to be met with haggard faces and complaints of a "really tough day." Although her parents often asked her about her studies and whether she had completed her homework, they had little energy to actually get involved in their daughter's education. Susan sadly recalls how her parents were even too tired to help her with a biology project one year.

Despite her parents' urging their daughter to pursue medicine or a similarly high-powered professional career, Susan equated higher education with only misery and fatigue. And why wouldn't she? Her parents were as successful academically as they could be, but they were always tired and unhappy. Why would Susan want to be like them?

Susan attended college and began dating an older artist halfway through her sophomore year. Months later, Susan announced that she had taken up painting and that her boyfriend had convinced her she was good enough to make a living off her new vocation. Since Susan had never picked up a paintbrush or shown any interest in the arts before, her parents were understandably worried. Despite their protests, Susan's mind was made up. She dropped out of college and married the artist. As it turned out, her parents fears were confirmed: her career as an artist floundered. Susan is now divorced and trying to get a degree in communications at a small community college.

So what went wrong? We are not saying that people with a love and talent for art should not pursue their dreams. Susan, however, chose to pursue that particular career path with little talent, drive, or understanding of what it took to be successful. Had Susan's parents shown her that education and learning provided (at least some) happiness, pride, and security, things might have turned out differently.

On the flip side, our friend Christy was the eldest daughter of two Chinese immigrants. Her father was an orthopaedic surgeon, her mother an electrical engineer. When Dr. and Mrs. Wong emigrated to the United States in 1973, Dr. Wong had already been practicing in China as an attending orthopaedic surgeon. Because of differences in medical licensing between China and the United States, Dr. Wong was forced to repeat his orthopaedic surgery residency in Pennsylvania. Although he had already completed the grueling residency in China, he and his wife decided that the advantages of practicing medicine and raising a family in the United States were well worth it.

Although Dr. Wong spent many of his nights away from home, he never complained. When he was home, he made a point of spending quality time with Christy. Although it would have been easier to come home and catch up on some well-deserved sleep, Dr. Wong chose to spend time with his daughter. Christy learned that her father loved taking care of his patients and that his happiness and pride were well worth the long hours and small salary. Christy is now completing her residency in general surgery and hopes to specialize in breast cancer. More importantly, she is happy and fulfilled by her career.

The sacrifices parents make—even the little ones—can have a huge impact on a child's life. We know parents who have purchased the smallest house in a great school district just so their children can reap the benefits of a good education. Others have forgone buying a new car so that their child could have brand-new textbooks. Children of parents who make these sacrifices are reminded on a daily basis how much their education is worth. These parents are not complaining about how much time and effort they are dedicating to their children's education. On the contrary, they are content with the knowledge they are doing everything in their power to ensure the best future for their children.

Secret 1: To-Do List

- You are your child's best role model, so be enthusiastic toward learning and education.
- Always create ways to actively include learning in your profession. This will dramatically increase your career advancement opportunities and add to your sense of professional fulfillment in a way that will benefit both you and your child.
- Surround your children with people who love learning and are in diverse fields. This will allow your children to develop a healthy respect for learning while also giving them information to pursue various career paths.
- A love of learning is imperative to success in any field and should be promoted with enthusiasm despite any objections you might have toward the professions your child wishes to pursue.
- In order to instill a love for learning and education in your children, you must 1) exhibit this love yourselves or expose your children to people who do portray this love, and 2) joyfully invest the time to teach this love to your children.
- Incorporate learning and education into all your children's activities so that they don't associate learning primarily with school or homework.
- Don't just tell your kids how important their education is to you—make the sacrifices in your lives that will convince them.

Secret 2

Instill a Sense of Family Pride and Loyalty

Regardless of culture, all children (and adults) want to feel loved and supported by their family. It is also safe to say that most children want to please their parents (at least initially). The difference between many Asians and many Americans lies in the value placed on individual achievement. Americans value individual success above all else, putting less emphasis on family and other support mechanisms. In Asia, success achieved by one member of the family is considered "one for the team"; in other words, the entire family shares the glory. Children are taught to excel for the sake of family pride.

Individuals pursue or crave success for a variety of reasons. Success is so alluring, those who experience its sweetness often crave more. It goes without saying that success is rarely achieved without the help of others. A good example of this can be found in AA, or Alcoholics Anonymous. Men and women in AA beat the odds mainly because other members in the group hold them accountable for their actions. In the group setting, individuals refrain from succumbing to bad habits with the help of many supporters. The encouragement and admiration from others serve as powerful positive reinforcements for success, and the potential disappointment to these supporters is a powerful deterrent to failure. Asian families work much the same way, in that success attained by any individual member is never credited to him or her alone. Because the entire family supported the individual in his or her endeavor, the entire family shares in the sweetness of victory.

Stress family, not individual achievement. Build accountability and loyalty by having the entire family celebrate successes of its individual members.

Our parents always viewed our family as a team working together toward a common goal. If any member of the family was struggling, the entire family would rally behind him or her. There were no "individual" successes or victories—only family accomplishments.

It was the simple things our parents did that worked. For example, we remember one year when Soo was having a difficult time with her high school chemistry class. She had recently begun attending the North Carolina School of Science and Mathematics (also known as NCSSM), an elite public school in Durham. Throughout the state, students gifted in the areas of mathematics and science applied for admission to this prestigious (and free) school. Only a handful gained acceptance, and Soo was one of the lucky few.

As always, with this honor came considerable hardship. Soo had always breezed through her science and math classes with little effort, but now she was struggling to maintain a B-minus average. The courses were much more challenging than she had ever imagined, and Soo was no longer at the top of her class. She was now amongst the best and the brightest in the state.

After receiving her first-quarter report card, it was evident that chemistry was her weakness. Rather than be discouraged, however, our entire family sprang into action. Since Soo lived at school during the week (all the students were required to), our parents had regular pep talks over the phone. On Friday afternoons, the whole family would travel to Durham to bring Soo home for the weekend. A scrumptious Korean feast would be served, and we would enjoy each other's company and spend time catching up.

The conversation would eventually focus on Soo's uphill battle with advanced chemistry. What always surprised us was the genuine fervor our parents showed tackling the issues. They were constantly asking how they (and even Jane) could help Soo improve her grasp of chemistry, and ultimately her grade. They also always made it clear that they expected only that Soo try her best, and if Soo was happy with her performance, so were they.

Initially, Soo was miserable. She was having difficulty understanding and hence applying the advanced concepts, and was becoming increasingly frustrated. Soo had always had a great (almost photographic) memory that had served her well in the past, but now the bar had been raised. She would have to fully comprehend all principles in order to perform well at this school, rather than simply regurgitate memorized facts.

Improving the way Soo tackled chemistry became a household project. After dinner and some relaxation and fun (usually a quick trip to the neighborhood Baskin Robbins), Soo would sit down with our father and review the material she had learned that week. Our father had been a chemistry whiz of sorts (at least that's what he says!) in the past and had been reviewing the concepts during the week while Soo was away. He had a deep appreciation for knowledge and believed that a thorough understanding of science and mathematics required extraordinary amounts of perseverance and time.

Together, Soo and our father would tackle chemistry problems. Soo often tried to come up with an answer quickly while our father tried to slow her down to ensure that she fully understood the material. Our mother would do her part by preparing tasty snacks, and Jane would do her part by staying in rather than going to the movies or the mall with friends so that she would not distract Soo from her goal. As you can see, Soo's individual goal of mastering chemistry truly became the entire family's goal.

And it worked. After several months of sacrifice, Soo's chemistry grade went from a B-minus to an A-minus. After she received her report card, we all celebrated our accomplishment (note that we say "our") by going to a nice steakhouse and the movies. The weekends returned to normal, with less intensive studying and more fun activities. In other words, the entire family reaped the rewards for Soo's accomplishment, because all had participated in achieving it. And Soo got to experience satisfaction on an individual level as well as on a larger scale. She had made the entire family proud and successful in its endeavor.

The lesson here is quite simple. No one ever makes it completely on his or her own. Instilling a sense of family pride and sense of duty, as well as a team work ethic, will hold your child accountable for his or her performance at school. Children will work harder and appreciate educational successes more if they believe that their actions affect their entire family, not only themselves. Contributing to both the happiness and sense of pride in the family can be a powerful incentive for children to put their best foot forward in school. In addition, children who see their parents and siblings making sacrifices themselves will develop a fierce loyalty to their families. This loyalty will often translate into a stronger commitment to educational excellence.

Teach your child that his/her performance at school affects the entire family by celebrating successes or addressing failures together.

Although Soo was a natural student who most of the time seemed to get straight A's with minimal effort, Jane was not. We'd like to reiterate that the point of this book is not to brag that Asians are far more talented than everyone else, or that Asians were born with the ability to excel in school. In fact, Asians are no more intelligent than their Caucasian, Latin, and African-American counterparts. As Jane's story shows, the difference lies in our upbringing.

Jane was born with several gifts, which included creativity, a desire to help others, and a knack for elaborate storytelling, both spoken and written. On the other hand, she was easily bored, particularly when it came to homework. After several years of schooling and standardized tests, it became clear to our parents (and Jane) that she was a smart girl—but she had to work for her academic success. Like the majority of us, she was certainly gifted in areas, but without effort or dedication to her studies, she was destined to be an average student. With effort and perseverance, however, she proved there wasn't much she couldn't accomplish.

Our parents were well aware of both Jane's gifts and weaknesses, and wanted to ensure that their daughter reached her full potential. Jane did well in grade school, bringing home above-average grades in most subjects and stellar grades in English and social studies. Our parents kept a close eye on the subjects she had difficulty with, and even Soo pitched in to help Jane grasp certain difficult concepts.

But Jane's struggle with her grades increased considerably in high school, when our parents moved to Tokyo and enrolled her in a competitive international school, The American School in Japan (ASIJ). ASIJ was considered a top-notch school, routinely sending almost all of its graduates to college and a good percentage to the Ivy Leagues. After her first semester there, Jane brought home a report card our parents had never seen before. Jane's report cards typically consisted of a pretty equal mix of A's and B's; this report card had only one A, several B's, and a couple of C's.

Our parents were initially shocked, then disappointed, and ultimately concerned. Jane had always managed to be an above-average student, and now her grades more reflected that of an average student. With these grades, Jane's chances of gaining admission to a reputable college did not look good. More importantly, it was clear that she was having difficulty grasping science and math concepts.

Although the academic difficulty and caliber of her high school played a factor in Jane's mediocre grades, another critical factor was that both our parents at the time were juggling demanding jobs with long hours. Since Jane had always brought home decent grades before she moved to Japan, our parents simply assumed this would continue throughout high school without much assistance from them. Boy, were they wrong! With our parents often leaving for work before Jane awoke and coming in past dinnertime most days, she had something she had never had before: plenty of unsupervised free time. For a normal fifteen-year-old like Jane, this meant time spent shopping with friends, watching movies, playing in the park, and doing anything *but* studying.

Our parents sprang into action. The first thing they did was meet with Jane's science and math instructors to hone in on the problem areas. With their help, our parents devised a plan of attack to improve Jane's grades. The plan involved dedicating a solid extra half hour to science and math after regular homework assignments were completed. Our parents both scaled back their hours at work and studied Jane's textbooks to refresh their memories, and together the three embarked on their journey. Even Soo, who was in the States starting college, spent time reviewing complicated science concepts with Jane during her Christmas and summer breaks.

You see, Jane's poor grades were not considered solely *her* problem. Both our mother and father felt that their daughter's difficulties in science and math were also *their* problem, and acted accordingly. Our parents had always instilled in us the value of family pride and loyalty, and never had the depth of their beliefs been more evident than at the time. Jane's ability to improve in the problem areas would reflect positively on the entire family, because the entire family would have invested their time and energy in pursuit of the same goal. Our parents believed that Jane owed it to her family to do her best at school; in return, our parents owed Jane their utmost devotion and assistance to complete the task.

Jane's grades did improve that next semester; her science grade went from a C to a B, her algebra grade from a C to a B-minus. Everyone was excited and enjoyed a sense of accomplishment. No one had expected Jane to get straight A's, but they had all hoped for an improvement. Each member of the Kim tribe had done his or her part to improve Jane's science and math abilities, which would eventually contribute to her overall sense of well-being, pride, and ultimately, her future. That was certainly a reason for the entire family to celebrate. There were no individual victories in our family, and for that we are grateful.

Having said that, Asian parents are also infamous for taking the idea of family honor and pride too far. On this note, we'd like to share a story our father once told us about a high school friend of his.

In Korea, all high school students across the country took standardized college entrance examinations. These examinations were individualized for each university; the most difficult tests were the ones that would determine acceptance into the most elite schools (which were and still are Seoul University, Yonsei University, and Korea University). Each university administered its own examination, and most elite schools' exams were held on the same day. Students attending smaller or more rural schools where the curriculums were less rigorous often performed worse than their peers attending larger city schools. Our father attended school in a rural village 100 miles south of Seoul, and although he fared well (he attended Yonsei), a colleague from the same neighborhood did not.

Unlike in America, where an aspiring college student can apply to as many colleges as he or she desires, students in most Asian countries have fewer opportunities for admission. As we said, the top universities hold their examinations on the same day, forcing students to choose which school's examination they will take. Although students who fail to gain admission still have the option of taking an entrance examination for a less prestigious or "second-tier" school, many of these students choose to study and wait an additional year in hopes of gaining admittance the second (or third or fourth!) time. Admittance to a top university considerably increases a student's chances of breaking into a certain field or profession, so most Asian students opt to delay their college careers a year or more in hopes of obtaining their degrees from the more prestigious schools.

Getting back to our story, our father went to high school with a boy named Jin Soo. Jin Soo was an average student with a tremendous work ethic. Being the only child of elderly parents, Jin Soo felt a lot of pressure to perform well academically. Despite urgings from his high school teachers to apply to a college where he could apply his talents and excel, Jin Soo opted to apply to Seoul University, Korea's most prestigious university.

Jin Soo studied diligently day and night, waking up at the crack of dawn and staying up past midnight in hopes of beating the odds. The day of the examination, an exhausted Jin Soo, along with thousands of other hopeful students, gave the test his best shot.

Weeks later, Jin Soo stood outside of Seoul University along with hundreds of other students who had gathered for an early glimpse of the list of accepted students. He anxiously waited his turn, but when he finally got the courage to look, his heart plummeted. His name was not on the list.

The walk home that day was the longest ever for Jin Soo. On more than one occasion he nearly lost the nerve to tell his parents the bad news. He hung his head as he rounded the corner to his house. As expected, his parents were on the porch waiting for him. Their expectant faces soon filled with sorrow as they witnessed their son's beaten expression. Jin Soo's mother immediately scurried into the kitchen to remove all evidence of a congratulatory party.

According to our father, the next week was a miserable one for the whole family. Both Jin Soo and his parents refused to leave the house for fear of running into friends or neighbors. A week later, Jin Soo ran away from home, leaving a note saying he was sorry he had brought shame onto his family and that they were better off without him. Rumor has it that Jin Soo wandered the countryside for days without food or water, praying to God he would not survive the ordeal. Fortunately, he was not granted his wish. Nearly a week after he ran away, a dehydrated and starving Jin Soo finally made his way back home. A year later he even gained acceptance into a competitive although not elite university.

You might find this story appalling, as we did. However, our parents insist that this type of reaction by the crestfallen student and his or her family was more typical than not. In Asian countries, gaining admission to a competitive university is the top priority of the entire family. When the student succeeds, the entire household celebrates victory; when the student fails, the entire family retreats and licks its wounds. Unfortunately, for some students who fail to achieve their goals, unrealistic or selfish parental expectations create an overwhelming sense of shame upon the family that is often too much for young adults to bear.

You are now probably a little disturbed, and understandably so. American parents tend to be much more encouraging when their children fail to meet expectations in the classroom. As a result, there are far fewer devastating emotional and physical consequences. Jin Soo's story was an example of what can go wrong when parents have unrealistic expectations. It also shows how the Asian mentality of bringing shame onto the entire family can be harmful when taken too far.

Developing a strong sense of family pride and loyalty takes time and considerable effort, but the rewards in the classroom and beyond are considerable. Again, teach your children that their performances at school are family efforts and that their successes (however small) will reflect positively on *the entire family*. Recently, Jane read an article about a young man whose dream since he was a young boy was to become a swimmer for the U.S. Olympic team. The young man recalled training day in and day out with his coach, who also happened to be his dad. He fondly remembered his dad coming home from work and driving to the pool where he would tirelessly critique his son's stroke and time his laps—often for hours at a time. Weekends at the pool often involved this ambitious young man's mother and sister cheering him on and pretending to be judges at the Olympics. Although this young man did not make the team (at least not yet), he has said repeatedly that his family's dedication to his dream instilled in him such a fierce sense of family pride and loyalty that has only fueled his desire to succeed more.

On a final note, we would be remiss if we failed to address the issue of cultural pride in this chapter. Although grateful to be in this country and proud to be Americans, our parents certainly never forgot their heritage. They never failed to remind us that we were members of the Kim clan and that being Korean was something to be excited about. Throughout our childhood we were taught to be proud of Korean traditions unique to our family and culture, and this sense of pride and originality has benefitted us both in and out of the classroom.

Build family pride and loyalty by stressing the uniqueness of your family in as many ways as you can.

Activities That Build Family Pride and Loyalty

- **Learn the national anthem of your country of origin.**
- **Learn some recipes specific to your country of origin.**
- **Trace your family name as far back as possible by creating a family tree.**

Andrea Jung, CEO and chairman of Avon Products, Inc., also shares our view that taking pride in one's culture can stimulate success. She writes, "As I reflect on my rapid rise to the top as one of the few women running a major global corporation, I have found myself thinking a great deal about my Chinese heritage and how enormously fortunate I am to have been given this very precious gift. I was raised in a traditional Chinese family where achievement was not demanded, but expected. My father, born in Hong Kong, was a successful architect. My mother, born in Shanghai, was the first female chemical engineer in her graduating class at the University of Toronto in Canada. They arrived in America not speaking a word of English but through hard work, both were able to fulfill their full potential, and their success has set a wonderful example for me. My parents were always, and continue to be today, the single biggest influence in my life. They raised my brother and I with a respect for the values and traditions of our Chinese heritage, yet also with an unwavering commitment to bring us up with all the opportunities for higher education and a desire to prepare us to adapt to American society and to succeed in this world of great change. My brother and I were given all the opportunities of our American friends—the same schools, the same tennis lessons, the same piano teachers . . . but we had the wonderful advantage . . . of a cultural heritage that we were always taught to be proud of." (Quote taken from a speech given by Andrea Jung at Guanghou University, China.) Don't make the mistake of raising your child to feel that he is one of many others just like him; take pride in your family by emphasizing your uniqueness, and watch your child's confidence and performance both in and out of the classroom grow.

Secret 2: To-Do List

- Stress family, not individual achievement.
- Teach your child that his/her performance at school affects the entire family by celebrating successes or addressing failures together.
- Build family pride and loyalty by stressing the uniqueness of your family in as many ways as you can.

Secret 3

Instill a Respect and Desire for Delayed Gratification and Sacrifice

We live in a country consumed by instant gratification and speed. Americans today have less leisure time than ever before, and we don't want to spend those few precious minutes waiting—for anything. American businesses, from Fed Ex to H&R Block to Jenny Craig, are constantly thinking of ways to develop and tout faster services and results.

Like most Americans, we are products of our environment—an environment consumed by instant gratification, speed, and wealth. Today, the thought of having to wait more than two minutes for a Big Mac at the drive-thru nearly puts Soo in hysterics; having to wait for more than a few minutes to purchase an item at Macy's irritates Jane beyond belief. However, we both managed to study diligently for years to obtain our medical and law degrees while many of our peers struggled to find the patience to complete high school or college. How were we able to delay gratification for greater rewards in the future while so many others were not?

Instilling a respect for delayed gratification and its rewards starts with the parents. We were fortunate enough to have two parents who were living examples of how working diligently and patiently for a long period of time was well worth the time and effort. Our parents firmly believed that rewards achieved over many years were much more satisfying than short-term accomplishments, and their lives always reflected this belief.

The story of how our father decided to come to the United States remains one of our favorites and perhaps best exemplifies why he so believed in the values of delayed rewards. Our father grew up in a poverty-stricken village 100 miles outside of Seoul, the capitol of South Korea. He was one of five children in a household that often had no running water. Red meat was such a luxury that only our grandfather regularly ate it. Our father, who loved a good steak, recalls vividly how our grandfather would tell his children that the only way to financial freedom was to excel in the classroom.

Well, our father took his advice to heart. Driven by dreams of a better life and the option to eat steak regularly, he worked his way to the top of his junior high, senior high, and college classes. Our uncles and aunts recall that he never complained about his late-night studies; the excitement about his future was so great. Our father carefully mapped out a plan to become a university professor in mathematics and computer science, fields he loved. In the end, our father even surprised himself by performing so well in college that he was offered a rare scholarship to study abroad and receive his master's degree in computer science at the University of Southern California. A little more than a year later, our parents celebrated their one-year anniversary at a steakhouse in Los Angeles. To this day, the food of choice at Kim family celebrations is steak.

Firmly believe that rewards reaped through hard work and diligence, however delayed, are more satisfying than short-term accomplishments. Set an example for your children by always leading your life according to this principle.

In addition to being living examples of how the greatest rewards are generally not easily obtained, our parents also offered us practical advice. "Always envision your end result," our parents would tell us time and time again. In other words, they recognized that it was tough for kids (or anyone, for that matter) to wait for more than a few minutes—much less months or years—for their rewards. They hoped that, by actively reinforcing the joy and fulfillment we would obtain at the end of the road, they would provide us with powerful motivators to get there.

Our mother is a great example of someone who helped herself achieve long-term goals by envisioning future success and happiness. Unlike our father or us, our mother did not achieve her professional goals until much later in life, putting her own desires on hold in order to maximize her daughters' chances at achieving their educational goals. Our mother took her role as an educator very seriously and did not want anything (including pursuing her own dream of becoming a computer science professional) to get in her way. She religiously taught us every night after school, and for hours on weekends. Those were hours she could have used to obtain her own degree in computer science, yet neither of us can remember our mother ever losing her patience with us or making us feel guilty for delaying her ambitions. Envisioning her future and all of its potential rewards always made our mother content.

We now know how difficult it is to sacrifice individual aspirations for the greater good. Our mother did this with a smile and without ever holding a grudge; the vision of two professionally fulfilled and financially independent daughters in addition to the vision of attending her own graduation ceremony one day were never far from her thoughts. When times got tough, thoughts of eventually walking across the stage with a degree in hand and going to job interviews as a more qualified and confident candidate energized her weary mind.

When Soo started college, our mother went back to school and received a degree in computer science. We recall the entire family watching with pride and gratitude as our mother finally walked to the podium in her cap and gown. Today a beautiful picture of our mother in a gray cap and gown with gold embroidery (she made the dean's list, of course!) sits in our living room and is a constant reminder of how great things can happen to those who wait.

Help your kids reach their long-term educational goals by teaching them to envision the joy and satisfaction their future successes will give them.

If you're still doubtful that your kids can learn to endure homework and after-school study sessions for years before getting their college or graduate school diplomas (just by following your example) take heart: it takes more than simply being ideal role models to help your kids delay gratification. Thankfully we have a few other tricks up our sleeve to share with you—ones that are practical and easy to implement.

Imagine that someone was to come up to you and ask you which of two scenarios you would prefer: the first scenario would have you living in a high-security prison for ten years, after which you would have a fun-filled and glorious life filled with love, fame, friends, family, and riches; the second scenario would have you living a comfortable and satisfied life (but nothing amazing like in the first scenario) your entire life. We'd dare to say that most people would pick the second option.

Indeed, most of our friends and family picked the second option for one main reason: despite the promised riches of the first scenario, the sacrifice and suffering preceding them were way too severe. In other words, no matter how much you may be promised down the road, no delayed reward will be worth it if you have to suffer considerably in the process. That's why it's important to enjoy the journey and have fun along the way, even if you are putting off your dreams. If you don't enjoy the ride, rest assured you'll never cross the finish line.

Our parents helped us do that by throwing in a few instantly gratifying experiences for us to enjoy while we were achieving our long-term educational goals. For example, we both spent numerous weekends over many months and years preparing for the SATs. As you can imagine, dissecting sample questions and reviewing test preparation booklets day in and day out can become extremely tedious, and we all know more than a few students who were unable to give this test the consistent, focused attention it deserved. Our parents realized that their daughters would not be able to study for lengthy periods of time effectively unless they were having some fun or enjoyment along the way. We recall taking fifteen-minute breaks after a seventy-five minute study session to play ping-pong or badminton. Sometimes our parents would structure our study sessions around a TV show we all enjoyed but often did not have the time to watch. At the end of a good study weekend, our parents always rewarded us for our efforts by taking us to the mall, a movie, or a restaurant (when money was really tight, we ordered Pizza Hut). By providing us with these "mini-rewards" along the way, our parents significantly increased our chances of reaching the finish line. Kids will be kids, after all. Just as you can't expect a two-year-old to sit quietly for two hours in a movie theater, you can't expect your kids to put in years of hard work with no reward simply by telling them to envision that pot of gold at the end of the rainbow.

Have fun along the way! Make sure the sacrifices your kids make on the road to academic success are not too severe; allow your kids to indulge occasionally in things that provide instant gratification.

Although it is necessary to give your child a few instantly gratifying experiences to maximize his educational success in the long run, never forget that true academic achievement and the fulfillment that it brings cannot be attained through a series of quick fixes. Your kids will catch on if you don't truly believe this. Everything you do and the way you live your life should exemplify the idea that education provides the most significant rewards when achieved over many years. If you're a single mother attending night school to obtain your degree and you show your impatience about having to wait three or four years to get it, chances are your child won't exhibit the patience necessary to get his. While you may concede to your child that many aspects of life are instantly rewarding, never put academic achievement or fulfillment in this category.

Teaching your kids to delay gratification for maximum future success is no easy feat, so like most things in life it's better to start early. Just as a child can easily master three or four foreign languages while an adult struggles to learn one, it's easier to teach a three-year-old to delay gratification than to break a ten-year-old's bad habits.

As you likely already know, teaching a child to delay gratification is not for the faint of heart. But it can be done . . . in a series of small steps that lead to big results. For example, every parent has experienced the humiliation of being in the grocery store checkout line when his child starts pleading for candy. And every parent (at one time or another) has reluctantly purchased candy as his child's pleas grew louder and louder. Well, we as kids were no different. We liked candy as much as anyone, and would often try to sneak Snickers bars and lollipops into the shopping cart at the checkout line.

In retrospect, we can hardly recall a time when we asked for candy and got it without some resistance. Our mother was always one step ahead of us, and taught us to appreciate delayed gratification in the process. The minute we arrived at the checkout line and before we could even start begging, our mother would turn to us and give us a big smile. "I have a great idea," she would say with encouragement. "If you two read one new book from the library this week, next time I'll buy each of you a candy bar." Before we could even start to ask if we could have one that day, she would ask us to pick out which candy bar we would want the next time around. Our mother was not one to back down (in other words, crying and screaming never got us the candy any sooner); believe it or not, we always voraciously attacked our assigned tasks and got our hands on the prize the next time. Somehow our mother managed to arrange grocery trips with us so that we ended up getting candy only about once a month, but we didn't care. We were having fun reading, learning, and anticipating that mouth-watering candy. Our mother taught us not only to delay gratification but also to associate delayed rewards with education and with greater satisfaction.

Don't just tell your kids to wait for great things—show them firsthand that patience will ultimately bring greater rewards. As a young girl, Jane loved to paint her nails a wide variety of colors. Soo recalls our mother occasionally granting her youngest daughter's wishes, giving her a manicure with great care. When she was done, our mother always told Jane to sit still for at least ten minutes to let her nails dry. Initially, Jane was unable to sit still before the polish had dried and would ruin her nails. She would then beg our mother to repaint them. Our mother always kindly but firmly refused—"Maybe next time you'll learn to wait until they dry," she would say. And learn Jane did . . . eventually. At the tender age of six, Jane would learn that by giving up ten minutes of her time she could enjoy her beautiful nails for weeks rather than mere minutes. You see how our mother had taught Jane to appreciate delayed gratification using something as simple as nail polish!

Our parents used tactics like this not only while we were young kids, but also much later in life. Soo recalls heading off to Johns Hopkins for college, where most of the students had cars. After her freshman year, she moved off campus and began pressing our parents for an automobile. Realizing that money was tight but wanting a car anyway, Soo compromised and asked if our parents could buy her a dependable but used car for several thousand dollars.

As you might have guessed, neither of our parents succumbed and bought Soo a car . . . at least not at that moment. Always careful to seize opportunities and create what our father loves to call "win-win situations," our parents told Soo that they would buy her a *brand-new* car once she gained acceptance into medical school. Almost immediately, Soo got over her initial disappointment and spent the next two years excelling in her classes. Two weeks after she received her acceptance letter to medical school, she received the keys to a brand-new, teal blue Toyota Tercel. Soo loved that car more than any single material possession, treating it to waxes and frequent car washes. She even cried like a baby when it broke down and had to be towed away years later. The point is, the car meant a lot more to Soo because she had worked so hard to get it. Similarly, your child's satisfaction and happiness will be much greater the harder and longer he or she works to fulfill his or her educational goals.

Teach your children the value of delayed gratification early by using practical scenarios even they can understand.

We've all heard the phrase "the family that eats together stays together." Along the same lines, we believe the family that sacrifices together stays together. Which brings us to our final practical tip: don't *impose* sacrifice and an appreciation for delayed gratification on your children. Rather, get your kids involved in deciding what the family will sacrifice to help them achieve their long-term educational goals. Family members who feel that their voices matter are far happier than those who feel their opinions are inconsequential. In addition, involving your kids in this process will provide them with a deep appreciation for how important their long-term academic achievement is to the entire family.

Soo remembers rather vividly one sacrifice the entire family made. The summer between her seventh and eighth grades was the summer that the entire family was to go to Disneyland. Our parents had been saving for quite some time and finally felt that they could comfortably make the trip. Three months prior to our trip, however, Soo was given the opportunity to enroll in Duke's Talent Identification Program (TIP), a three-week course for gifted middle schoolers. She had scored a 620 on the math portion of the SATs while she was only in the seventh grade, and participating in TIP would allow her to take an advanced mathematics, science, or computer course. Soo, who often sat nearly bored to tears in even her advanced seventh-grade math class, desperately wanted to go. Our parents also wanted her to go and be challenged, but there was one catch—the course would cost them almost two thousand dollars.

Two thousand dollars was a lot of money. After reevaluating

their finances, our parents came to the conclusion that we could not both go to Disneyland *and* send Soo to Duke that summer. It would have to be one or the other.

Like many other times, our father called a family meeting. These meetings typically consisted of the four members of our family sitting around our small dining-room table and staring at each other until our father announced the agenda. Usually, because the meetings seemed so unnecessarily formal, neither of us could keep a straight face for very long.

Our father always liked these meetings to resemble a sort of forum, or fake courtroom. Like a judge presiding over a courtroom, he commanded our undivided attention as he relayed to us the family dilemma. In this case, it was that our family had enough money to either send Soo to Duke or send the entire family to Disneyland. All members of the family would vote, but in the event of a split decision (2–2), our father (the "judge") would have the final say.

We always started with the youngest member of our family, Jane. She was only in fourth grade at the time and had been dreaming of Disneyland for more than a year. Despite being torn and wanting Soo to be happy, in the end Jane voted for the family to go to Disneyland. The vote next turned to Soo, who also voted that the family go to Disneyland. Although she wanted to attend the camp (thoughts of having fun with students her own age without her parents were dancing in her mind), she couldn't allow the entire family to forego their vacation plans on account of her. In addition, Soo also had been eagerly looking forward to going on the family vacation.

Our mother opted for Soo attending the camp and the family taking a more local (cheaper) vacation. After her vote, all eyes turned to our father, who concurred with our mother. Given the split vote, it soon became clear that our father would have the final say. Sensing defeat, Jane's eyes began to water as her images of amusement rides and cotton candy began to disappear.

In the end, our parents happily sacrificed a week-and-a-half, long-deserved family vacation to Disneyland in order to send their eldest daughter to Duke that summer. They did it with joy, happy to provide a wonderful educational opportunity for Soo. On the other hand, they didn't forget that the entire family deserved a nice vacation. After Soo returned from her three-week camp, our family went to a local amusement park, where Jane stuffed her face with cotton candy and hot dogs. Later that summer, we also spent a few days at Myrtle Beach, a short drive from our house in North Carolina. We all played in the sand and the ocean, got golden tans, and feasted on all kinds of junk food we were normally not allowed to eat. To this day, Soo will think of all the fun she had (in addition to all she had learned) during those three weeks at Duke and become misty-eyed with gratitude for the entire family's tremendous sacrifice and insight. Being involved in the decision-making process had also increased Soo's awareness of how important her education was to the entire family and strengthened her commitment to her academic growth.

Jane also recalls a particular occasion when she was included in making a difficult decision regarding her education. After successfully implementing a systems network in Tokyo, our father was asked to take on a similar project in Malaysia when Jane was a junior in high school. Although our parents had enjoyed their stay in Japan, the demands of their jobs in addition to long hours were starting to take their toll. Moving to Malaysia would offer them a more relaxed lifestyle for two years, after which they could return to North Carolina and see old friends.

In the usual Kim family format, our father called a meeting. This time, Soo was not present, since she was attending college in the States. During this meeting, our father informed Jane of the opportunity to work in Malaysia for an additional two years—an opportunity he wanted to take. He mentioned it had been a tough decision for both him and our mother, but they believed it was time to move on.

The move would occur that summer, with Jane just one year shy of graduation. When asked how she felt, Jane could not help but express her disappointment and sadness in not being able to graduate from her current high school. The international high school Jane attended in Tokyo had an outstanding academic reputation and faculty; many of its graduates were accepted to Ivy League schools and its alumni included renowned artists, scientists, professors, and authors. Jane had also made many close friends, and having been uprooted once three years earlier, she was not looking forward to leaving her friends behind and adjusting to a new school and country.

After a series of discussions where the pros and cons were discussed, our parents and Jane decided that she would remain in Japan to complete her high school education. Jane would spend six months living with her best friend Shannon and her family, and would obtain her high school diploma before returning to Malaysia. Our parents' decision showed Jane just how dedicated they were to her education and academic development, and also just how much they cared about Jane's happiness. It was no easy feat for our somewhat overprotective parents to allow their little girl to live apart from them before college, not to mention in an entirely different country! To this day, Jane is grateful to the Bohm family for taking her in and treating her as one of their own. She would also like to thank them for allowing her to take the last train home every now and then, and failing to mention this to her parents!

Include your kids when deciding what to sacrifice for their long-term educational goals.

The key to achieving success long-term (in education as well as in other endeavors) lies in always seeing the big picture and delighting in the small sacrifices you make along the way. When our parents first came to this country, they lived in a small one-bedroom apartment that quickly became too crowded for a family of three (Soo was born shortly after our parents came to the United States). Nonetheless, they made it work. When they moved to Montreal so that our father could work for Northern Telecom (now Nortel Networks), they lived in a similar apartment that was way too small for a family of four (Jane came along soon after the move). Somehow, they made that work too. While many of their peers splurged on material possessions, our parents pinched pennies and clipped coupons while living modestly. Although many of their peers attempted to overcome their disenchantment with life with cheap thrills and material possessions, our parents focused all their energies on raising two happy, educated, motivated, and successful daughters. While many adults their age attended dinner parties and social engagements while leaving their children in the care of babysitters, our parents stayed home with us and taught us the importance and joy of learning on a daily basis.

Our parents had the mentality that any sacrifice, no matter how small or large, was well worth the delayed rewards of possessing a top-notch American education. They had the battle scars to show for it, as our father had been willing to leave all of his friends and family behind to pursue a master's degree in America, a country he had only read about. Witnessing our parents live happy and fulfilling lives despite their sacrifices strengthened our drive to commit to years of higher education, which were at times grueling.

From what we could tell, sacrificing for delayed rewards was a great way to live. Our parents never complained when they spent hours helping us with our homework instead of watching TV or relaxing. Not once did they frown when they had to cancel their plans in order to drive us to various school activities.

Looking back, our mother and father are far happier having two educated, well-adjusted, and independent children than they ever could have been if they had opted to splurge on designer clothes and extravagant vacations. They deliberately chose to focus and spend on our education and practically eliminated the possibility of ending up with two deadbeat daughters. They enjoyed their roles as parents and had fun raising us despite the hard work, discipline, and sacrifice they endured along the way. Today, their lifestyle is quite different as they travel, dine at great restaurants, and play golf twice a week. However, we still have fond memories of the countless Saturday afternoons our family spent together at the library.

Secret 3: To-Do List

- Firmly believe that the rewards reaped through hard work and diligence, however delayed, are more satisfying than short-term accomplishments. Set an example for your children by always leading your life according to this principle.
- Help your children reach their long-term educational goals by teaching them to envision the joy and satisfaction their future successes will give them.
- Have fun along the way! Make sure the sacrifices your children make on the road to academic success are not too severe; allow your kids to indulge occasionally in things that provide instant gratification.
- Teach your children the value of delayed gratification early by using practical scenarios even they can understand.
- Include your children when deciding what to sacrifice for their long-term educational goals.

Secret 4

Clearly Define Your Child's Role as a Student

We all assume certain roles in society: teacher, doctor, lawyer, plumber, homemaker, etc. Imagine if there were an abundance of lawyers but no garbage collectors. What if everyone decided they wanted to be a carpenter and no one wanted to be a doctor? If no one went into law enforcement, there would be chaos.

Just as a community needs people in different roles to function well, a family also needs its members to carry out different duties in order to get all the "work" done. Thankfully, the roles for men and women are no longer restrictive and rigid, and they continue to evolve. Women are no longer the primary homemakers, men no longer the primary breadwinners. Today, women are making strides in the workplace, and men in turn are enjoying the wealth and are pitching in more at home. Childrearing, in the past solely the woman's responsibility, is being shared more equally in today's hectic two-career or single-parent households.

Children's roles have changed less drastically: most parents simply want their children to be happy, healthy, and responsible. Nevertheless, it seems that kids in America today are doing more than ever. They are parents' helpers (doing chores around the house), participants in extracurricular activities that can include several sports and/or musical instruments, and students. In this day and age of increased single-parent homes, many children are also assuming the responsibility of parent/guardian for younger siblings or confidant/substitute spouse for their single parents. As children today juggle more and more responsibilities against a background of more distractions (the Internet, cable television, etc.), it is only natural that school performance and dedication to education suffers.

Needless to say, the more clearly defined and simple one's role is, the more likely one is to perform well. In other words, if you expect your child to assume numerous roles, chances are that he or she will not excel in any one of them. Children in Asian families tend to have more clearly defined roles than their American counterparts, and we think this is another reason why Asians tend to excel in the classroom. While American children are splitting their time between a million different extracurricular activities in addition to helping run the household, Asian students are concentrating on their studies. By and large, the role of Asian students in the family is clear-cut and only two-fold: 1) respect your elders and obey your parents, and 2) study hard and do well in school in order to secure the brightest future you can. Asian parents stress the role of student and knowledge-seeker more than their non-Asian counterparts, with good results in the classroom.

Our parents firmly believed in roles, and they made sure that each member carried out his or her role to the best of his or her abilities. Our father was the breadwinner during the day, an educator at night. Our mother kept the house and finances in order during the day, and also became an educator at night. Our role during the day was to obey our teachers and excel in the classroom. Our role at night was to obey our parents and excel in our continued studies at home (i.e., homework, additional studies supervised by our parents). Of course, we also pitched in around the house, cleaned our rooms, did the dishes, and enjoyed learning and playing tennis with our father.

All children acquiesce to their role as students during the day as they spend the daylight hours in the classroom under the watchful eye of teachers. After school hours, however, many children eagerly adopt other roles, wishing to break free of books and boredom. Children today equate the final ring of the school bell with freedom from learning and education. Therein lies the difference between many Asian-American children and their peers.

While many non-Asian children flock in droves to the sports fields, malls, or local restaurants to blow off steam after hours, their Asian counterparts are heading home earlier. While many non-Asian children are barely making it home for dinner and then are hurriedly attempting to finish homework (sometimes while watching TV), Asian children are reviewing their homework with their parents and preparing for class the next day. Of the non-Asian children that do head home after school, many spend hours in front of the television, barely breaking for dinner before they reunite with the tube. In Asian families, education and learning do not stop after children come home from school—in fact, they have only just begun.

The majority of non-Asian children view their roles in the classroom and at home very differently. These children know that they are to study while at school; however, but they see home as a place where they can unwind and forget that school ever happened. Because they themselves were not taught that the role of student is one to be assumed during *and* after school hours, many parents allow their children to forget about learning as soon as school ends.

The majority of Asian children never shed the role of student.

Regardless of their roles during the day, Asian mothers and fathers automatically assume their dual roles as parents and educators at night. Most Asian parents take their roles as educators as seriously as they take their roles as parents, and their children reap the benefits of going the extra mile. None of the great thinkers/inventors/scientists of our time became as successful as they were simply by doing the bare minimum. If Albert Einstein only studied and pursued his dreams during school hours, rest assured his name would not be recognized today. Imagine how much less he would have accomplished had he simply turned his brain off after three o'clock every afternoon, and every weekend.

Asian parents do several things that allow their children to effectively embrace the role of student. For one, they strictly manage their children's time outside of school. Second, as we pointed out, Asian parents gladly assume the role of educator after school hours (those who are the most effective assume this role after collaborating with their children's teachers). Third, Asian parents (with the help of their children's educators) teach their kids that being a student is both fun and rewarding. Last but not least, Asian parents possess a genuine respect for teachers; never would they undermine an educator and allow their child to believe that being a student is anything but a privilege, or that the role of student is anything but a coveted one.

Spend at least one hour doing homework with your child every night.

Asian parents appear to keep a much closer eye on their children than their non-Asian counterparts, both inside and outside of the home. Many of our non-Asian friends have commented on how strict our parents were with our time after school. Afternoons spent at the mall or hanging out with friends were extremely rare. Completing schoolwork was a prerequisite to even *asking* our parents to do something other than school-related activities after school. As a result, we grew accustomed to making schoolwork and education our top priority even after school let out.

Our parents managed our time after school so well that our daily routine was utterly predictable. Most days, our mother would expect us to come home directly after school. Over snacks we would talk about our day, kick off our shoes, and relax. If the weather was nice we would go outside and play badminton or softball. About an hour later our mother would sit down with us at the dining-room table as we discussed any upcoming tests and/or assignments that were due. For the next hour and a half (with one ten-minute break) we would complete all of our homework. As soon as our father came home, the four of us would sit down and have dinner together.

Our studies, of course, did not simply end at dinner. After clearing the table and washing the dishes, we would resume another one to two hours of "study time." Activities during this time would not involve mandatory homework, but rather go far beyond what was expected: during this time we might get a head start on our summer reading list or attempt to learn concepts beyond what our homework assignments might have tested. Our father always loved to check our homework, after which he would make up five to ten much more difficult questions for us to answer, just to make sure we truly understood what we were doing. If either of us had a test the next day, our parents would quiz us to determine how well we had prepared. Today we are amazed at the level of enthusiasm, patience, and energy our parents possessed. They always actively pursued being the best educators they could be. Between our school instructors and our "home instructors," we felt like we were learning twenty-four hours a day!

Manage your child's time after school carefully. Establish a strict yet enjoyable schedule or curriculum after school hours in order to constantly reinforce the role of student in your child.

This may sound obvious, but having a good relationship with your child's teachers is the key to setting the stage for his success as a student. This is especially true when your child is young, as younger children have incredibly limited attention spans that require near-constant stimulation. Talk with your child's teacher about which activities and methods of teaching your child is most receptive to—trust us, it will save you time and energy when it comes to adopting your own teaching style at home. By all means, don't feel the need to recreate the wheel! Who has the time? Use what works for your child's teachers—professionals who have spent years studying the minds of children!

Getting your child to embrace being a student also involves individualizing methods of learning that will best work for him. In other words, what works for one child may not work for another. After frequent meetings with our teachers and working with us on a daily basis, our parents soon realized that their daughters enjoyed very different styles of learning. Soo learned best independently and disliked studying in groups; she thrived on competition and often put her best foot forward when the competition was at its fiercest. Soo never did have a problem focusing on the prize and going for it, regardless of the stakes. Jane's learning style, however, could not have been more different. Jane thrived in group settings where concepts were discussed thoroughly and issues raised and dissected; always slow and steady, Jane disliked external pressure or competition. Our parents thus employed the element of competition more frequently with Soo; with Jane they stressed discipline and perseverance to achieve educational goals.

Assume the role of educator after school hours so that your child can't shed the role of student at home. Incorporate styles or methods of teaching that your child's educators believe are most effective for him.

Most children will rebel at the thought of assuming the role of student both at school and at home; the trick is to make them believe there is no greater job to have. Children will embrace the role of student and knowledge-seeker if they learn that this role is both fun and rewarding. This, of course, starts in the classroom. Educators who take the time to get to know their pupils individually and attempt to make their classroom dynamic and interactive can better reinforce to students that the role of student is a coveted and privileged one. These educators encourage free speech and free thinking, staying away from boring assignments in favor of more exciting projects that will teach the same concepts.

We salute the many teachers and educators who have raised the bar and made the extra effort to make learning even the most mundane of concepts interesting. These men and women work hard despite little financial reward and at times, little respect from their students, to fight for what they value most (the development of young minds).

The first teacher to leave an indelible impression on Jane was Mr. Noonan, her first-grade teacher. Mr. Noonan was a soft-spoken man, yet his passion for conveying knowledge to his students was extraordinary. Like any seasoned speaker, Mr. Noonan knew his audience. He understood that first-graders had low attention spans, were prone to fidgeting, and became bored easily. All his lessons had a common denominator, which was active student participation. He never lectured for more than five minutes at a time and taught his lessons via skits, mock game shows, and question-and-answer sessions.

One class project Jane remembers vividly involved learning about other nations and their cultures. Each group of five students would pick a nation to represent and would be responsible for researching and sharing with the class the food, language, and customs specific to their country. The enthusiasm for this project was so overwhelming that Mr. Noonan decided that the class should perform a show for the parents at the end of the year. During the show, exotic foods were tasted, new languages were learned, and numerous culture-specific customs appreciated. Needless to say, the class got a standing ovation at the end of its performance.

Just as great teachers like Mr. Noonan are able to transform mundane assignments into ones that are both fun and knowledge-generating, great parents (or "after-school educators") are able to do the same. Our parents did their best to make us feel that being a student every weeknight after dinner was enjoyable. Concepts were never crammed down our throats; rather, they creatively and ingeniously made their way into our minds.

As a parent, making sure that your child's educators are helping your child embrace being a student starts with establishing a collaborative and mutually respectful relationship with them. Parents and teachers need to view themselves as partners—partners whose mutual goal is to make their kids excited about being students. That can be accomplished by regular meetings where both parent and teacher recognize their mutual pupil's strengths and weaknesses, and together devise methods to best help him or her enjoy being a student. In other words, make sure that your child's educators are making learning fun! Our parents routinely met with our instructors and learned quite a bit from them in the process; it was not unusual for our parents to use the same tactics at night our teachers used effectively during the day, and vice versa!

Teach your child that being a full-time and lifelong student is both rewarding and fun.

Lastly, your child will respect his role as a student only if he believes his educators are respected in their roles. In other words, if your child gets wind that you believe his teacher is ineffective, there is little chance he will embrace being that educator's student. Today, America's teachers are getting less respect from parents than ever before. In one survey, 73% of new teachers expressed that parents treat schools and teachers as adversaries (*TIME* Magazine, February 21, 2005). If you're not on the same page as your child's educators, how can you possibly stress to him the importance and privilege of being a student in the classroom, much less at home?

In sharp contrast to America, teachers in Asia are treated with the utmost respect (this will be further discussed in Secret 5). Most Asians view disrespecting a teacher as tantamount to disrespecting royalty, and our parents were no exception. Although many American parents find it difficult to separate their beloved child from the poor or struggling student in the classroom, Asian parents have little difficulty doing this. While many American parents are quick to defend their children against what they often feel are personal attacks by educators, most Asian parents are working together with their children's educators to analyze and solve their children's problems.

As we mentioned earlier, Jane often struggled with her science classes in high school. One year after Jane brought home two below-average test scores in biology, our parents decided it was time to schedule an appointment with Jane's teacher, Mr. Chaiken. Prior to the meeting, Jane had attributed her poor grades mostly to Mr. Chaiken himself, stating that the biology teacher was considered one of the toughest teachers in school—someone who reveled in giving students bad grades. Jane also credited her poor performance to Mr. Chaiken's teaching style, which she described as too rushed. After listening to Jane's comments, our parents decided to take an afternoon off work the following week to meet with Mr. Chaiken. Rather than barraging him with questions about why Jane's grades weren't better and why he was flying through material too quickly, our parents gave him the opportunity to objectively analyze Jane's performance. And how far from the truth Jane was! For starters, Mr. Chaiken mentioned that Jane often appeared distracted or bored in class. Although he agreed he moved quickly through the material because there was so much to cover, he was quickly able to convince our parents that he gave the class ample opportunities to ask questions in class or to schedule one-on-one appointments with him after hours. Despite Jane's struggles, not once had Jane bothered to ask Mr. Chaiken questions or schedule an after-school meeting with him to pinpoint problems or address difficult concepts.

After the meeting, our parents then sat down with Jane to share what they had discussed with Mr. Chaiken. Soon they had Jane admitting she had little interest in biology, which made it difficult for her to concentrate in class. Her indifference had caused her to fall farther and farther behind, forcing her to cram for tests rather than steadily reviewing and reinforcing the material.

Now fully understanding both sides of the story, our parents collaborated with Mr. Chaiken to develop a plan of attack. First, Jane would have to relearn any principles she had failed to master. Jane would meet with Mr. Chaiken once a week to review difficult material and ask questions after school; at home, Jane would review the day's lesson and explain concepts to either Soo or our parents to demonstrate that she fully grasped them. Over the course of several weeks to months, Jane's test scores steadily improved. And by siding with Mr. Chaiken, our parents showed Jane that they would do nothing to compromise her role as *his* student.

Show the utmost respect for your child's educators; never undermine an educator and compromise your child's ability to be a student by turning the teacher into an adversary.

In summary, never let your child shed the role of student. Being a student is a lifelong, full-time job, and a rare privilege. Getting your child to embrace his role as a student will not happen overnight; in fact, it may be closer to a lifelong endeavor. Once accomplished, however, you will have given your child a priceless gift: the fulfillment and achievement that comes with being a lifelong seeker of knowledge.

Secret 4: To-Do List

- Manage your child's time after school carefully. Establish a strict yet enjoyable schedule or curriculum after school hours in order to constantly reinforce the role of student in your child.
- Assume the role of educator after school hours so that your child can't shed the role of student at home. Incorporate styles or methods of teaching that your child's educators believe are most effective for him.
- Teach your child that being a full-time and lifelong student is both rewarding and fun.
- Show the utmost respect for your child's educators; never undermine an educator and compromise your child's ability to be a student by turning the teacher into an adversary.

Secret 5

Cultivate a Respect for Elders and for Persons in Positions of Authority

If you think about the three people American kids idolize most, who comes to mind? J. Lo, Beyonce, and Madonna for young girls; Michael Jordan, P. Diddy, and movie stars like Colin Farrell for young boys. Young Americans today shower pop icons and movie stars with the utmost respect, but give government leaders, parents, and teachers little to none.

Flipping through cable television, we are bombarded with TV segments on celebrity icons; shows on *E!* and *Style* depict just how glamorous the lives of the rich and famous are. And as Americans, we love to watch. "Look at J. Lo," Soo heard one teenager say to her mother after she was told that without a college education she was not likely to get a personally and financially rewarding job. "She didn't even go to college, and look at her now." True as that may be, success stories such as J. Lo's are few and far between. What they don't tell you on those shows is that many dancers who started out like J. Lo are still working for peanuts and becoming increasingly disenchanted with their lives.

Our obsession with celebrity makes it acceptable for American children today to idolize those with fame, fortune, and good looks rather than those with intelligence, strong moral backbone, stalwart character, and commitment to education and the community. Why go through years of schooling to become the President of the United States to make only two hundred thousand dollars a year, when you can make a million per flick doing something a lot less stressful and more fun? Why go through years of schooling to become a nurse, working twelve-hour shifts for sixty thousand dollars, when you can sing and dance in front of a sold-out crowd for millions? Showcasing the world of the elite and make-believe, television has invaded American homes and has destroyed far more than our time. Parents must strive to counteract its influence by teaching children to revere our true heroes: the people serving others in society, whether it be a doctor, teacher, or simply a parent.

Limit the amount of time your children spend watching shows on channels like MTV and E!. Make them understand that pop icons aren't the norm.

While Americans idolize celebrities, children in Asia are taught from a very early age to respect—almost revere—three groups of people. First and foremost, elders are considered respect-worthy, as bearers of years of experience and knowledge (this group of people includes, but is not limited to, parents). Government officials also command the utmost respect, as leaders of the country. Third, children are taught to respect and obey all educators, from kindergarten teachers to college professors (we can just hear all you educators sighing right about now!).

Of course, we're not suggesting that Asian kids don't love

celebrities—Brad Pitt may be more popular in Japan than in the United States. However, this adoration does not typically invade the homes or schools of Asian children, as it does in America.

Although we would all rather help our children develop a healthy respect for their parents and educators than cultivate a respect for pop icons and movie stars, this is not easily accomplished in America. Despite our upbringing, as teenagers we still drooled over Ralph Macchio in *The Karate Kid* and wished we could look and dance like Janet Jackson. We're not saying that it's abnormal for children and teenagers to be star-struck. On the other hand, if your children are paying more attention to MTV and VH1 than to their teachers, you've got a problem on your hands.

As you've probably guessed, helping kids develop a healthy respect for parents and educators (rather than pop stars) starts in the home. In Asia, many children live in multigenerational households. Often, a married couple will live with at least one set of parents (typically the husband's parents—Asia is still a patriarchal society) in addition to their children. Relatives also tend to live nearby (in the same town or apartment complex, even), which exposes children growing up to a wide variety of older adult influences.

As we said before, the first thing Asian children learn is to respect their elders. The older the individual, the more knowledge and wisdom they have, and the more they are to be revered. The Korean language, in fact, allows for different ways of saying the same thing, depending on the age of the individual one is addressing. A more polite, respectful way of speaking is indicated when one is speaking to someone older (even when they're only three years older, which annoyed Jane); a more carefree tone and language is used in addressing a younger individual.

Parents are obeyed first and foremost. However, grandparents and senior citizens are also given the utmost respect, as individuals who have experienced an entire lifetime of trials and tribulations. Talking back to one's parents is unheard of, and forget about disobeying them.

We were reminded of how inherent respect for elders is in the Asian culture when we threw a party for our father's sixtieth birthday. Most of the guests were Korean, and when the invitations were sent, Jane was surprised to see that her name was listed below her brother-in-law's (Soo's husband, Joe) among the hosts of the party. When Jane pointed out jokingly that our mother had mistakenly put Joe's name above hers (after all, she was our father's daughter and was footing half the bill for the party!), she was surprised to find out that this was no mistake. Our mother went on to explain that in Korea, it was customary to list the name of the eldest child first in any correspondence followed by his or her spouse. Younger children would be listed below that of their older brothers- or sisters-in-law, simply because they were born later. Respect for elders is strictly upheld in all Asian cultures and permeates all customs, however big or small.

Asian culture is one rich in rituals and formalities (more so in the past, but many persist). Adults bow to each other in greeting, careful to exhibit only the highest respect for their fellow man. Indeed, many Asian traditions embody the importance of respect, particularly to elders, which fosters obedience and discipline. But while Asian culture emphasizes sacrifice, obedience, reservation, and humility, American culture exalts those who exhibit independence, confidence, and an opportunistic or entrepreneurial spirit. In America, children's self-serving or unruly behaviors are frowned upon, but often not aggressively stopped. The media also significantly influences and shapes America's young minds. After all, the role models in America are the most outspoken individuals, the ones oozing confidence (even arrogance). In Asia, self-serving or rowdy behavior is immediately halted, not only by the parents, but also by the child's older cousins, aunts, uncles, and grandparents. Unlike their American counterparts, Asian role models are typically more reticent, humble, and mild-mannered.

Never tolerate disrespect for elders or authority figures from your child, whether it's reflected in his tone, language, or behavior.

Just about now you may be thinking that Asian ideals tend to stifle leadership and independence in children. After all, why would anyone choose to teach their children to be meek and submissive when we want our children to become leaders rather than followers? Rest assured, possessing a respect for elders and those in positions of authority does not suppress independence or individuality. On the contrary, instilling in your children a devout respect for educators and those in positions of authority will only improve their educational experience. Once this groundwork is laid, there is no limit on how much your child can achieve with the tools they have mastered.

Jane got the opportunity to experience firsthand the difference between an Asian and an American classroom. As we mentioned earlier, Jane attended an international school in Tokyo, Japan. Although students came from forty-seven different nations around the world, the majority of the students were Americans whose parents were expatriates and Asians whose parents had either returned to Japan and could not reenroll their children into the Japanese school system, or who desired their children to experience a more American education (mainly to become fluent in English!).

Jane's Japanese language class consisted of a roughly equal mix of Asian and American students. Her teacher was a matronly woman with a quick wit and a thick accent named Sensei (Japanese for "teacher") Yamamoto.

Sensei Yamamoto ran a tight ship—there was to be no eating or chewing gum in her classroom. If any student spoke without being called on, his or her name would be written on the blackboard. If this happened three times throughout the course of the semester, the student's grade would immediately be bumped down a half a letter grade (for example, from a B to a B–, from a B+ to a B). After several students suffered from demoted grades as a result of talking out of line, Sensei Yamamoto finally got her respectful, obedient classroom. This all changed when *Andrew* entered the picture.

Andrew was an American whose parents had recently transferred to Tokyo via IBM. He was inattentive, could barely keep his head up in class, and was almost always unprepared. Five weeks into the semester, he had already had has name printed on the blackboard a whopping eight times—and actually seemed proud of it. Andrew burped often, deliberately dropped his books to create distractions, and made annoying whistling sounds whenever Sensei Yamamoto turned her back.

Jane recalls a particular day when Andrew went too far. At the time, the high school was in the midst of a student government election frenzy. The buzz surrounding the elections was so intense that even Sensei Yamamoto, normally not one to discuss social events in her classroom, took a few minutes to talk about the intense race. "How does everyone feel about the election?" she asked once students had settled into their seats, her thick Japanese accent causing her to pronounce the word "election" as "erection." After an uncomfortable silence, harsh, cynical laughter could be heard from the back of the room. "I'll show you an erection!" Andrew snorted, nearly doubled over in hysterics.

Pretty soon, about half of the class was laughing along with him. Even Jane, normally a polite and well-behaved student, had to stifle a chuckle. But a few minutes later the laughter did die down, particularly when students witnessed the hurt expression on Sensei Yamamoto's face. Jane also quickly noticed that the students who had not participated in the laughter seemed outraged by those who had; it soon became apparent to her that many of the students who had refrained from showing Sensei Yamamoto disrespect were Asian, while the vast majority of the other students were American.

The story is not meant to illustrate that American students are rude and disrespectful while Asian students are models of exemplary behavior. Rather, it portrays how differently American and Asian children are raised to view their educators. In Asia, educators are viewed as noble individuals dedicated to the education and enlightenment of their pupils. In sharp contrast, there are very few students in America who view their educators as more than authoritative figures standing in the way of a good time. In America, the class clowns (or the most disruptive students) tend to be the most popular; on the other hand, students in Asia who behave in this manner are often ostracized by their peers.

Shaping how your child views educators is one of the most important things you can do as a parent. Educators in Asia are considered among the brightest individuals and are revered for being altruistic enough to dedicate their lives to passing their knowledge to the next generation. Long before an Asian child enters grade school, this respect and admiration is deeply engrained in his heart and mind.

Instilling a respect for elders and educators starts in the home. Children should be taught early on that respect for their elders is not simply appreciated but expected. Many families have chosen mealtimes to instill this respect, making sure that children don't interrupt their parents or grandparents while they are talking. Enforcing good table manners and polite speech also goes a long way both at the dinner table and at school—rarely do you see a child who misbehaves atrociously at home not duplicate this behavior in the classroom.

The best way to get your children to respect their educators, though, is to speak positively about them at all times. There is no place for derogatory comments about your child's educators in your household—if your child suspects you have little regard for his teacher, he will learn to share your disdain. Even if you question the educator's teaching methods or competence, sharing these concerns with your child rather than the school administration will only do your child a disservice. Make treating elders and educators with the utmost respect and admiration a priority in your children's lives. Your children will be better people and better students for it, we assure you.

Asian students are generally considered among the most quiet, obedient, and respectful students in any classroom. If you think that this behavior, particularly in this day and age, does not go a long way in the eyes of the weary, sometimes fearful, and grossly underappreciated educator, think again. We have had numerous educators inform us that it was their pleasure to teach us. We listened intently to their words, handed in our assignments on time, and did our best to lead by example. We never encouraged nor condoned those students who tried to gain popularity with other students at the expense of our teachers, nor did we befriend those who routinely caused chaos in the classroom with rude behavior.

It's okay to encourage your child to be the teacher's pet! Handing in quality work on time, being attentive and courteous in the classroom, and encouraging the same behavior from peers will win the hearts of your child's educators. Rest assured your child will reap the benefits for years to come!

The important thing to remember is, showering teachers with the respect they deserve will help your child succeed—it certainly did wonders for us. We can't count the number of occasions that our educators went the extra mile for us, both professionally and personally. If we had a dime for every time one of our teachers took extra time after school to explain a particularly difficult concept to us, Soo would be able to purchase a whole new wardrobe. If we had a quarter for every time a teacher took the time to offer advice on the college admission process and how to beat the odds, Jane would be able to do the same. If we had a dollar for every time a teacher wrote us a letter of recommendation or made a phone call in support of us to a potential college, graduate school, or employer—well, you get our drift.

And the rewards don't end in the classroom. Our ability to treat our educators, friends, parents, and colleagues politely and respectfully has furthered our careers and won the hearts of friends and family. We would not dream of doing things differently.

Secret 5: To-Do List

- Limit the amount of time your children spend watching shows on channels like MTV or E!. Make them understand that pop icons are not the norm!
- Never tolerate disrespect for elders or authority figures from your child, whether it's reflected in his tone, language, or behavior.
- It's okay to encourage your child to be the teacher's pet! Handing in quality work on time, being attentive and courteous in the classroom, and encouraging the same from peers will win the hearts of your child's educators. Rest assured, your child (and indirectly, you), will reap the rewards for years to come!

Secret 6

Play an Active Role in Your Child's Education

Parents are busier than ever these days. In many families, both parents work; almost all single parents hold down at least one job. As we mentioned before, the last thing any hard-working man or woman wants to do after a long day's work is to struggle through homework with their child or discuss strategies to improve SAT scores. However, the worst thing you can do as a parent is to put your best foot forward at your day job and neglect a job far more important—one that involves educating your child. Long after you're gone, your workplace will have forgotten you. On the other hand, if you commit yourself to playing an active role in your child's education, your child (and their children!) will reap the rewards of your efforts for years to come.

The first thing to do is to meet regularly with the men and women who are educating your child during the day. Ignore the protests and groans from your child and get on a first-name basis with his or her teacher. Start as early as possible (even kindergarten or pre-school), and make these meetings a top priority. Try to schedule an introductory meeting within the first month of each new school year. It is surprising to us how many men and women never fail to miss a weekly staff meeting but can't find the time once a month to meet with their child's teacher, even for a few minutes. Your job pays the bills and offers personal satisfaction but your children are your legacy! We suggest you set up monthly meetings with your child's teacher—frequent enough to develop an open and intimate relationship with the teacher without putting extreme time constraints on both you and your child's educator.

The monthly meetings should be friendly, relatively brief and to the point. You may want to chat with your child's teacher for a few minutes before you badger him or her for information on how little Luke is doing with his ABC's; remember that teachers are people too, not just vehicles by which your son or daughter will gain admission to Harvard. The more your child's educator likes you as a person, the more he or she will like your child. Although teachers hold themselves to high standards and try to be impartial, they are only human. If you are rude or pushy with them, chances are they won't go the extra mile for your child in the classroom.

After breaking the ice, mention topics brought up at the previous meeting. If your child's teacher thought your son or daughter needed to improve in a particular area, bring it up first thing. Briefly outline what efforts you personally have made to work with your child, and ask the teacher if she has noticed results. If she has, you can pat yourself on the back. If she has not, ask her how she thinks you might be able to bring about improvement.

It is important to always look for ways in which your child can improve. Teachers are a wonderful resource, and if you have developed an open and comfortable relationship with them, they will likely talk freely about both your child's strengths and weaknesses. A mistake many parents make is to be offended by a teacher's comments or suggestions. If you want to hear only about how well your child is excelling in all aspects of his social and academic education, don't even bother to schedule these monthly parent-teacher meetings. In fact, just stay home and watch TV—at least you'll be well rested.

Next, bring up new areas in which your child could improve. Be open and direct with the teacher; make it clear that you appreciate her efforts to mold your child into the best student he or she can be. Take notes, and keep them together in a notebook; highlight the "Areas for Improvement" and "What we're doing to ensure improvement" sections. By keeping a journal, you will be able to tell whether your methods or techniques are working. If you notice the same thing listed under the "Areas for Improvement" section after months have passed, you'll know you need to switch strategies or enlist outside help.

It's important for parents to convey a desire for improvement at these meetings. Parents who want to hear only about their child's successes are doing the child a serious disservice, and are denying themselves an invaluable resource: the teacher. Be humble and realistic about your child's accomplishments. Your child (and every child) has room to improve in the classroom, and by openly discussing these areas with his or her teacher on a regular basis, you can rest assured that they will be addressed.

Of course, you needn't only focus on the negative. After you briefly discuss areas that need improvement and possible strategies to bring about change, focus on the positive. Find out what areas your child seems to excel in and how you might further encourage these strengths. Remember, praise and encouragement are powerful motivators for everyone, but particularly for children.

During parent-teacher meetings, be prepared to discuss your child's weaknesses openly and without taking offense. Keep a list of what you discussed at each conference. And don't forget to take a moment to celebrate your child's successes!

After each meeting, set aside some time to talk to your child about his or her performance in school. If possible, do it in a fun family setting. As we mentioned previously, we grew up with all the essentials but very few of the extras—we had plenty of food, clothing (not designer, mind you), and shelter, but not much else. Going out to eat was seen as a waste of money, and rarely occurred, despite all of our protests. Our parents, however, did make one exception. After each monthly parent-teacher meeting, the four of us would head to Pizza Hut, our favorite restaurant. Over hot breadsticks and a large Supreme pizza, our parents would summarize their discussion with our teachers. The message was always clear: they were proud of us and knew we were doing well, but there was plenty of room for improvement. To this day we view those nights at Pizza Hut fondly, even though most of the conversation centered around educational goals. We learned early on that discussing and formulating a plan for continued education and growth could be rewarding and even fun. And we felt good about knowing how involved with our education our parents were. They cared enough about our future to meet with our teachers often, they respected us enough to include us in developing strategies for improvement, and they loved us enough to spend $19.95 plus tip to treat us to our favorite food. How lucky could two girls be?

Make an effort to appear excited about parent-teacher conferences; if possible, time them to coincide with a fun activity with your child.

Of course, it is much easier to meet with a teacher on a monthly basis when there is only one person involved in your child's education. After elementary school, meeting with five or six different teachers for different subjects every month is nearly impossible. After your child completes grade school, stick to your goal of monthly parent-teacher meetings, but meet with teachers of major subjects on a rotating basis. If there is a particular subject that your child is struggling with, choose to focus your energies on meeting with that teacher more often than the others. Remember, the goal is to play an active role in your child's education, not drive yourself (and the teacher) crazy by juggling an unmanageable schedule.

Playing an active role in your children's education also involves staying on top of their grades. This means knowing exactly when they get their report card. To this day, it amazes us that our parents always knew when our report cards went out. We couldn't even put off showing a less than stellar report for a day.

Soo recalls rather vividly one particular afternoon in her seventh-grade year. She had just received her report card, which to her astonishment contained far more B's than A's. Although this was certainly not a poor performance by any standards, Soo knew she had not given her best performance that quarter. She was trying hard to fit in, and it was tough being the only Asian kid trying to make her straight black hair curl in front like Heather Locklear's. Soo's grades had slipped because of a lack of focus. She knew our parents would be disappointed because she hadn't done her best.

On the all-too-short bus ride home that day, Soo decided to put off showing our parents her report card until after the weekend. It was already Thursday, after all, and a little procrastination would spare her a lecture and even spare her parents a rotten weekend (at least, that's how Soo rationalized her little white lie).

Determined to carry out her plan, Soo immediately joined Jane in the kitchen and began pigging out on freshly baked cookies. Our mother followed her every move, her black eyes inquisitive.

"So how'd you do?" our mother asked with a smile after Soo downed her third cookie.

Soo shrugged with as much nonchalance as she could muster, her heart fluttering wildly in her tiny chest—after all, lying did not come naturally to her. "What do you mean?" she managed to say.

"Didn't you get your report card today?" our mother asked with a frown.

Soo should have known that an eleven-year-old, albeit a smart kid, was no match for our wise mother. But like most preteens, she thought she could pull a fast one. "No, I didn't get it today," she replied coolly. "I think it's coming Monday."

Our mother remained silent, which at the time Soo interpreted as acceptance. To Soo's relief, her report card was not mentioned again that evening.

The next afternoon, Soo again pondered her options on the bus ride home. She could come clean, but that would ruin her entire weekend. And although she could handle our parents' disappointment and the inevitable lecture on how "they came to America so that their children could lead a better life," why should she ruin the weekend for the whole family? If she showed our parents her report card on Monday, Soo could suffer in silence and be the true martyr.

That day our mother met Soo at the door. "How was your day, honey?" she asked, her smile less bright this time.

"Fine," Soo replied, her heart heavy with the anticipation of lying again. "How was yours?"

"Good." Our mother's eyes narrowed a touch. "Anything special happen today?" she then asked pointedly.

"Not really," Soo said softly, surprised to see no signs of dinner yet. "What are we eating for dinner?"

"Your father just called and said he was going to pick up Pizza Hut on the way home," our mother replied cheerfully.

Soo licked her lips, her brave façade already beginning to crumble. "That's nice, Mom. What's the occasion?"

"Your sister did really well on her report card today. How'd you do?"

"I don't know yet," Soo replied nervously, having anticipated this question on the bus ride home. Jane was three years younger than Soo and still in elementary school—there was no reason that both schools should hand out report cards simultaneously. "I told you I'm not getting it until Monday."

Luckily for Soo, our father arrived with an aromatic pizza before our mother could grill her any further. Ten minutes later, Soo was on her third slice of pizza and her second Coke when our father burst her bubble.

"Soo, I don't know why you are lying to us about your report card," our father stated, his eyes sad. "Your mother and I know you got your report card yesterday. What are you trying to hide?"

Soo was so startled she nearly choked on a piece of sausage. "I didn't want to ruin your weekend," she blurted out, her appetite now dead. "I didn't want you to be disappointed in me."

"I am *very* disappointed," our father answered, "that I have a daughter who would lie to her parents rather than face the truth. If you did poorly this time, there's a reason for it. As your parents, it's our job to help you figure out what that reason is, and to correct it."

After the initial shock and embarrassment wore off, Soo reviewed her report card with our parents over dinner. Looking back, that Friday afternoon taught Soo a powerful lesson. There would be no pulling the wool over our parents' eyes when it came to any aspect of our education. It's clear now that their active involvement made us more diligent students.

Find out exactly when your child should get his report card, and make a point of reviewing all report cards as a family. This will stress the importance the entire family places on the education of its individual members.

Another important thing for parents to do is to help kids prepare well in advance for critical academic milestones such as standardized tests. Procrastination rarely leads to good things, particularly when it comes to scholastic achievement. It takes time to thoroughly learn and grasp concepts, and the more time you can spend with your child on educational activities, the better.

The best example we can give you of a critical milestone that requires lots of advanced preparation is the Scholastic Achievement Test, better known as the SATs. As you are well aware, all high school students applying to college take the SATs. As the only part of the college application (i.e., report cards, letters of recommendation, personal statements) that is standardized, SAT scores are routinely given considerable weight during the college admissions process. Although we realize that some schools are starting to steer away from SATs, the fact remains, an exceptional SAT score can only help your child's quest for admission. Furthermore, preparing vigorously for the SATs will help kids down the road when it comes time to take graduate-school entrance exams.

Which is why we are surprised that so many high school students don't give the SATs the attention it deserves. The application deadline for most colleges usually falls in the early spring of a student's senior year, although many colleges have early application programs that require applications to be submitted as early as November or December. Because SAT scores are not available for several months after test administration, most high school guidance counselors recommend that students interested in attending college take the test at the end of their junior year.

Although most students are aware of the important role the SATs play in the college admissions process, very few, in our opinion, prepare for it adequately. The vast majority of students will take the test at the end of their junior year for the first time. If they are not happy with their score, some will retake the examination in the fall of their senior year. Some of these students will enroll in popular SAT preparation courses over the summer hosted by Kaplan or the Princeton Review, hoping to drastically improve their score the next time they take the test. Although a select few manage to improve their score dramatically, most do not.

Asian students, on the other hand, tend to prepare for this examination as if their lives depended on it. Having grown up in a society where a child's entire future and profession are determined by a series of examinations, Asian parents have a healthy respect for standardized tests such as the SAT. Our parents were no exception. After learning of Duke's Talent Identification Program (also known as TIP), where middle school students who scored high on the SAT were eligible to attend advanced summer classes at the prestigious Duke University, our father purchased the Barron's SAT preparation guide for Soo while she was only in seventh grade. Several months later, Soo took the SAT for the first time as a seventh-grader and to our parents' delight, scored high enough on the math portion to obtain a scholarship to the summer program (you'll recall, the same program for which we cancelled the Disneyland vacation!). Her verbal score, on the other hand, was nothing to write home about.

After Soo returned home from the three-week summer camp, our father sat Soo down and again praised her for doing so well on the math portion of the SATs. After making it clear that she had much to be proud of, our father asked her if she felt she was having difficulty with vocabulary or reading comprehension. Soo adamantly denied any such difficulty, stating that her grades in English had always been excellent. Our father could not deny this fact, but the poor verbal score was staring him in the face. After careful thought, he encouraged Soo to complete the Barron's SAT manual he had purchased for her earlier that year.

By the end of her freshman year, Soo had completed all of the exercises in the book. Like a few other students who wanted a shot at the National Merit Scholarships, Soo took the PSATs (preliminary SATs) during her sophomore year in high school. When the results became available, Soo was once again surprised when her verbal score lagged far behind her math score.

We're not going to bore you again by sharing why our father chose the book *Jane Eyre* to get Soo to improve her vocabulary and reading comprehension skills. Suffice it to say that the active role our father played in working with Soo to improve her academic weaknesses paid off handsomely.

The key to acing standardized tests is repetition; take the tests as many times as possible, as far in advance as possible!

By playing an active role in your child's education, you are laying the groundwork for his or her success. It certainly is no secret that "practice makes perfect." The more time and energy you invest in your child's education, the more likely your child will take his education seriously. The more clear you make it that his education is your top priority, the more difficult it will be for him *not* to make it his.

We know parents who took this secret one step further, with great results. Not only did these parents guide their children in the right direction by encouraging educational activities and making them readily available—they actively participated in the activities with their children! Amanda, a good friend of Jane's from law school, shared a particularly touching story about the lengths her father went to to show his daughter that her education was his top priority. Much like our parents, Amanda's parents encouraged her to prepare for the SATs well in advance of her junior year. When it became obvious she was having difficulty with the math portion of the test, her father took the time to sit down with her and explain the more difficult concepts. And as we alluded to earlier, he didn't just stop there. When it came time for Amanda to take some practice tests, her father actually took them with her!

In the first chapter, we mentioned that our father also read many of the books Soo read to increase her vocabulary. By doing this, our father clearly demonstrated that he found the exercises worthwhile and stimulating. As a result, Soo found the at-times boring or mundane activities more interesting and rewarding; after all, if her father was willing to spend his precious time relearning concepts he was no longer required to know, they had to be important.

Soo's close friend Stephen, a surgeon and assistant professor at the University of Pittsburgh, shares similar stories of active parental involvement. Despite being a cardiac surgeon, his father never tired of working with Stephen on what his family considered their top priority—their children's education. Stephen recalls that his homework assignments always had to be carefully organized and neatly presented in order to be met with approval by his discerning father; mathematical and scientific problems and questions were to be carefully approached and analyzed. Stephen's father took great pleasure in working through everything from simple algebra word problems to complex differential equations, sitting with his kids while they worked through homework, waiting to help break down a problem into its simplest components. The active role Dr.

Lai played in his children's education, coupled with the enthusiasm and energy he was always able to muster, still impresses Stephen to this day.

Playing an active role in your child's education does not have to involve endless hours spent poring over books and examinations. Another way parents can participate is by encouraging and allowing their children to attend educational courses, camps, and programs. Investing some of your hard-earned dollars toward educationally related activities can go a long way in showing your child where your priorities are. It is amazing to us just how many parents would rather purchase the latest model of a car than invest in their child's education and future.

We mentioned earlier that Soo attended advanced summer courses at Duke University while she was in middle school. Although we were considered a lower-to-middle class family back in those days, our parents never scrimped on our education. Nor did they hesitate to spend money on extracurricular activities such as piano and tennis lessons. The message we received growing up was simple—our education was our parents' top priority and the one thing our parents would consistently invest their time, energy, and money into. The best thing you can do for your children is to provide them the same message.

Make investing financially in your child's educational opportunities a top family priority.

Which leads us to a rather interesting fact. Among our Asian friends and colleagues, parents had strikingly similar views when it came to investing in their children's educational activities. Money was never an issue (within reason, of course), and like us, they remember summers filled with camps, classes, and various programs.

Some came from wealth, others were middle-class, others were downright struggling to make ends meet, but none of them had any reservations when it came to spending money on their children's education.

Attending classes after school, on weekends, or in the summer is not a new concept to many first-generation Asian immigrants. For students in Asian countries such as Japan, Taiwan, Singapore, and South Korea, attending supplemental classes in addition to regular schooling is a part of everyday life. At a very early age, Asian students attend these classes in the hopes of gaining admission to a top university. One explanation why many first-generation Asian parents seem more apt to encourage and enroll their children into these types of classes is they themselves were used to attending them as children. Extra classes were familiar, even expected.

We said it before and we will say it again: *practice makes perfect.* Additional class time focusing on difficult concepts will put your child in a better position than the neighbor's kid who sits in front of a Playstation all afternoon. As parents, you have a unique opportunity to make sure your child sees the opportunity to learn in everything he or she does.

Secret 6: To-Do List

- During parent-teacher conferences, be prepared to discuss your child's weaknesses openly and without taking offense.
- Keep a list of what was discussed at each parent-teacher conference.
- Take a moment to celebrate your child's successes!
- Time parent-teacher conferences to coincide with a fun family activity.
- Know exactly when your child should get his report card and make a point to review all report cards as a family. This will stress the importance the *entire* family places on the education of its individual members.
- Prepare for standardized tests well in advance—years in advance, if possible.
- Make investing financially in your child's educational opportunities a top family priority.

Secret 7

Determine and Develop Your Child's Individual Talents

> **"There are tens of thousands of professions in this world. Every profession is unique. Every profession needs a few who are the best, who can develop and improve that profession. Why not pick an area within your limits, then set the goal of no limit for that profession. Within that area you choose, choose to strive for the best."**
>
> **—Dr. Henry Lee, forensic scientist on the O.J. Simpson case**

We see it everyday—the high school football star who pushes his son to play football professionally, the attractive mother who pushes her four-year-old daughter into modeling before she's even old enough to know what the word "model" means. We all know fathers who push their sons to become the physicians they were unable to be, the mothers whose unfulfilled dreams or passions translate into unreasonable and unwanted demands and expectations on their own daughters.

Although it is normal and healthy for parents to want the best for their children, some parents put an overwhelming amount of pressure on their children to become things they're not meant to be. On a professional level, no parent hopes that their children will grow up unemployed or disenchanted with their jobs; all parents hope their children will find secure positions that are personally fulfilling, intellectually challenging, and financially secure. On the other hand, parents often find it difficult to strike the delicate balance between guiding their children to these ideal professions while still allowing them the freedom to choose their own career paths.

You may be wondering whether we were victims of parental pressure to enter the medical and legal professions. After all, it is no secret that Asian parents often want their children to enter such professions—jobs with security, financial reward, and prestige. The truth is, our parents did significantly influence the professions we chose to enter. Not only did they encourage us to pursue these careers, they were convinced that our individual talents were best suited for the medical and legal fields.

From an early age, Soo was drawn to science. She recalls fiddling with the game *Operation!* for hours on end, intrigued by the human body and its various systems. She loved to work with her hands, playing with her toy stethoscope, enchanted by how a man-made tool could allow a person to solve the mysteries of the human body. One of her favorite childhood photos captures her at the early age of three, a colorful stethoscope around her neck and a doctor's bag in her hand.

She also had a knack for science and math. All the IQ tests and other similar evaluations pointed to the fact that her mind was well equipped to learn and solve science and math problems. She grasped concepts in these areas easily, with minimal effort (unlike vocabulary and reading comprehension skills, as you learned earlier). In school, she was able to complete exercises that were years beyond her grade level. Because she was gifted in the sciences, she naturally enjoyed studying those subjects more than the others.

Our parents, of course, were well aware of their eldest daughter's gifts. Wanting to develop these talents, they encouraged Soo to enroll in advanced classes and extracurricular activities that would both challenge her and further nurture her natural abilities. (As we mentioned previously, Soo's high score on the mathematics portion of the SAT enabled her to attend a prestigious summer camp at Duke University.) Soon our parents began to discuss with Soo various professions that would best showcase her natural talents; these included medicine, engineering, accounting, and computer programming. Soo, who had always been intrigued by the human body and enjoyed working with people, eventually gravitated toward medicine. As parents, it's important to pay attention to your child's strengths and areas of interest early. Don't be afraid to consult with his or her educators if you're having trouble identifying them yourself.

Soo's talent for science and math as a child took her to the North Carolina School of Science and Mathematics (NCSSM), a public high school for gifted students our father had researched long before Soo became a student there. It was at NCSSM that an anatomy class confirmed Soo's desire to become a surgeon. Her challenging course load also more than amply prepared her for the introductory pre-med courses at the Johns Hopkins University in Baltimore, Maryland. During her freshman year in college, Soo aced her classes and brought home a 3.9 grade point average. Three years later, she gained acceptance into the Johns Hopkins School of Medicine, a feat our parents were pleasantly surprised by.

Identify your children's natural talents and provide them with opportunities to enhance and nurture those abilities. Do your best to foster a passion for the fields that showcase your children's gifts.

Although Soo's path to becoming a surgeon was relatively straightforward and pleasant, Jane's path to becoming a lawyer was much stormier. As a child, Jane's individual talents were not as readily apparent as her older sister's. Unlike Soo who excelled in math and science, Jane's natural abilities lay in her storytelling and writing. She loved to conjure up stories (she was also prone to exaggeration because of this trait) and had a knack for reading and writing, which her educators and our parents also noted fairly early on in her schooling.

In stark contrast to Soo, Jane's aptitude for science and math was subpar; on the other hand, she showed considerable promise in the areas of creative writing, reading comprehension, social studies, and history. Her creative writing skills did not go unnoticed, and before long Jane's nonfiction and fiction works were being displayed in various middle and high school publications.

Our parents were excited and delighted about Jane's knack for telling a good story, although they were more than a little concerned about what direction her passion for storytelling might steer her. Images of a starving writer living in a closet in New York City haunted them. They were well aware that for every successful writer, there were thousands of other writers starving while trying to get their big breaks. Although our parents wanted to encourage Jane to follow her dreams, they also wanted her to pursue a profession she enjoyed that would guarantee her a steady and reasonable income. Knowing about Jane's interests in cultural studies, our parents encouraged her to obtain her college degree in international relations. Knowing that a degree in that area would provide numerous opportunities for writing, our parents believed they had found a way Jane could follow her dream while at the same time allowing her to develop skills that would be useful in more mainstream professions.

After graduating from the American School in Japan, Jane enrolled at George Mason University, a college with a strong international relations undergraduate program. Jane spent the first two years there predominantly taking international relations classes and a few writing courses. She continued to write on her own, publishing a couple of her essays and stories in newspapers and literary magazines on campus. Halfway through her college years at George Mason, Jane decided to transfer to the University of North Carolina at Chapel Hill. UNC Chapel Hill was closer to our parents and was considerably cheaper as Jane would be eligible for in-state tuition.

Jane continued to pursue a degree in international relations at Chapel Hill, but it soon became clear to everyone close to her that she had no set plans after college. Although her heart was in social work involving the underprivileged and immigrant populations, she was disheartened by the limited job prospects available to her. After researching the job market at length with her university's career counselors and our parents, she was still uncertain of where her talents and interests would be best served. After four years of college studies and months of pondering the heavy "What am I going to do for the rest of my life?" question, she was emotionally and physically exhausted. Not wanting to make a hasty decision, she decided to take a year off after college to discover her true interests.

Although our parents supported Jane's decision to take some time off, they were not about to let their youngest daughter spend the year in front of the tube or at the mall. After sending Jane on a European vacation where she got some much-needed R & R, they sat down with her for a serious talk. After congratulating Jane on achieving her hard-earned college degree, they set about defining her talents and interests. Jane's gifted storytelling and writing had always been appreciated by our parents, and they were proud that she had been able to further refine her skills while in college. Our parents also realized that Jane had a great heart and that she would never be happy in a job that didn't directly involve dealing with the less fortunate or underprivileged. Lastly, our parents understood their daughter's international interests—Jane loved studying and immersing herself in other cultures.

For the next few hours, our parents and Jane discussed at length how she could combine her unique talents and interests in a profession that would also provide her a decent income. She could be a writer, as Jane had always received accolades for her short stories. On the other hand, both Jane and our parents were well aware of the hurdles facing an unpublished writer trying to make an honest living. With no guarantee of a sale or hefty advance (we now know how tough the publishing business is, even with a star agent!), even Jane had to admit that the job of full-time writer was less than ideal. She also seriously entertained becoming a social worker, but the additional schooling for little financial gain (social workers are grossly underpaid!) was a turnoff.

After several lengthy and at times frustrating discussions with their youngest daughter, our parents eventually brought up the idea of law school. Law school required students to be adept writers, and with a law degree there were endless possibilities to significantly impact the underprivileged and/or immigrant populations. Last but not least, a law degree would assure Jane some financial security, even if she chose a job in the nonprofit or government sector.

Talk openly about your child's professional plans and encourage careers that will allow him or her to showcase talents while offering financial security. Put a limit on the amount of time off your child can take, and during that time, schedule regular meetings to discuss future plans.

Needless to say, Jane was initially horrified by our parent's suggestion. Still burnt out from her college studies, the thought of enduring three additional years of intense schooling was almost appalling. Furthermore, she hated "ambulance chasers" (probably because of her sister's profession) and had often viewed lawyers as unethical, smooth-talking individuals that would sell their soul if the price were right. A few months and a several hundred discussions later, however, Jane began to see the logic in the choice. Perhaps she *could* have it all.

As it turned out, the decision to attend law school was one of the best decisions Jane ever made. After applying to several law schools in the northeast, she was accepted and decided to enroll at Temple University. We'll be honest with you—as all first-year law students are well aware, the year wasn't exactly a picnic. Jane initially struggled, overwhelmed by the heavy and difficult class load. There were even times she doubted her decision to attend law school, particularly when she was pulling all-nighters trying to complete her torts assignments. To make matters worse, Jane was so busy that she had little time (or energy!) to write.

With the encouragement of our parents and Soo, Jane buckled down and got through that miserable first year. During her second year, she began working at an immigration law firm part-time. There she learned the ins and outs of the business and met countless immigrants who benefited from her services. Now in her element,

Jane rejoiced in applying the knowledge she had obtained in law school to practical issues facing the indigent immigrant population.

When Jane finally graduated with her law degree and secured a position at The Children's Hospital of Philadelphia as an immigration specialist, she had no regrets. She had found her niche—not in the courtroom, but in the field of immigration. During her final years at Temple, her experience working with various immigration practitioners whetted her desire to aid an immigrant population that was often burdened with language barriers and poverty. In the end, law school provided Jane with the opportunity to display her language skills and indulge her love for international affairs and cultural diversity—all while helping others and making a decent salary! As for her writing, Jane wrote more prose during her law school years than in all of her high school and college years combined. Now that she has more time, Jane's love of writing has resurfaced with a vengeance in the form of this book!

Many kids associate "secure" professions (i.e., medicine, law, engineering) with years of arduous schooling and difficult, albeit financially rewarding, lifestyles. Show your child that those kinds of jobs need not be devoid of creativity, flexibility, and fun.

Our parents were not the only ones playing an active role in their children's future livelihood. Christina Park, a CNN news correspondent, fondly remembers how her parents readily exposed her to a myriad of activities to determine her individual talents. She says, "One of the many things I'm most grateful for is how my parents opened my eyes to the world. As important as grades and studying were in my family, my parents made sure to immerse us in as many extracurricular activities as our curiosity and interest could hold. They showed me a limitless universe, full of dreams and possibilities. Nothing, they told me, was impossible or beyond my grasp. To this day, I still believe them. I cannot recall an afternoon coming home from school when there wasn't something to do. While most of my friends came home to watch TV (or perhaps dabble in some homework and play), my brother and I were constantly challenged to use our God-given talents, hone them, and excel. Even when money became tight, my parents never skimped on our education. I had unlimited access to books, which were the doorways to my imagination. My parents gave me so many gifts in the form of life lessons about working hard and believing in a dream. They sacrificed everything for us. I work hard to ensure that their work was not in vain." Christina Park's parents realized the importance of identifying their daughter's individual talents and nurturing them for maximum success.

It is certainly no secret that Asian parents want their children to pursue professions that are both prestigious and financially rewarding (more about this in a later chapter). On the other hand, Asian parents tend to steer their children away from careers or professions they feel offer little financial or job security, and therefore considered "high risk." Our parents firmly believed that many years of intense schooling and education would afford us skills that would single us out and make us marketable in more "low risk" and at the same time more intellectually fulfilling professions (i.e., business, medicine, law). While our parents have a considerable respect for writers and artists, they knew far fewer starving surgeons and lawyers than starving writers and artists.

Parents are among the few people who have only the purest and best of intentions for their children. If you, as parents, are not willing to identify your children's individual talents and guide them along the right paths, no one else will. You may be met with resistance, and ultimately your children may choose other paths than the ones you might have thought best for them. In the end, however, being able to nurture your children's talents and allow them to make informed decisions regarding their professional careers will be reward enough.

Secret 7: To-Do List

- Identify your children's natural talents and provide them with opportunities to enhance and nurture these abilities. Do your best to foster a passion for fields that showcase your children's gifts.
- Talk openly about your child's professional plans and encourage careers that will secure your child's interest and showcase his abilities while offering financial or job security. Put a limit on how much time off your child can take; during this time away from school or work, schedule regular meetings with your child to form and talk about his future plans.
- Many kids associate "secure" professions (i.e., medicine, law, engineering) with years of arduous schooling and difficult lifestyles. Show your child that these professions need not be devoid of creativity, flexibility, and fun.

Secret 8

Set Clearly Defined Short-Term and Long-Term Goals

Despite what many of our friends think, our parents did not sit us down when we were young and tell us that we were expected to attend top-notch colleges and become professionals. Although this is what they desired, our parents had enough common sense to realize that method might backfire. After all, children are not programmed to think twenty years down the road—as we all know from experience, instant gratification is what they desire. Just as you can't prevent your children from desiring a McDonald's Happy Meal by telling them they will thank you later for limiting such high-fat foods, you can't make your children excited about education by telling them they'll be grateful years later when they're making the big bucks in satisfying careers.

So what's a parent to do? How can parents fight and resist their child's desire for instant gratification . . . and win? The answer, put simply, is to provide a series of well-researched short- and long-term goals. And by short term, we mean very short term—think hourly, daily, and weekly for younger children, weekly, monthly, and yearly for older ones.

Our mother was one of the many moms who made the most of her children's short attention spans and came out victorious. As you know, our mother was a stay-at-home mom who cherished her time spent with her children—thinking of ways to make even the most mundane educational activities fun was a challenge she always welcomed. When we were very young, our mother viewed our minds as blank slates; she and our father had the privilege of deciding what to write on those slates. The challenge was, we were capable of focusing our attention for no longer than fifteen minutes (at most) at a time.

Not that our mother viewed our limited attention spans as significant obstacles—before we reached two years of age, she dazzled us with colorful storybooks. As soon as we began speaking (at the age of one according to our father, one and a half according to our mother), she introduced the alphabet to us. Starting from the letter "A," our mother went through each letter of the alphabet with us individually. She made a point to differentiate upper from lower cases, although we're not sure this concept really sunk in until we started school. Initially we concentrated on only two letters a day—one in the morning and one in the afternoon. After having us repeat the letter several times, our mother would write down a series of words (typically objects, for reasons that will soon become clear) starting with that letter. For example, for the letter "A" she might have written down the words "apple," "ant," "artichoke," and "animal." After reciting the words with her, we would then be given the task of locating the objects throughout the house. If we didn't have the particular object in the house (we were never allowed to have a pet, to Jane's disappointment), a picture of the object or word could be substituted. That was the part of the game we loved; we still possess vague memories of foraging through the refrigerator to retrieve apples or running around outside trying to locate ants (it wasn't hard).

Our mother's short-term goal for her toddler daughters was

simple: try to learn two letters of the alphabet a day. Every two weeks, the alphabet cycle would repeat itself. The game worked: we learned the alphabet quickly, but more importantly, we learned a ton of new words in the process. According to our parents, Soo knew that "candy" started with a "C" way before her second birthday.

Although our mother involved us in activities that lasted for only an hour or two at a time, she never lost sight of the big picture. At the end of the year, she wanted us to have learned the entire alphabet, upper and lower case. She also wanted us to be able to incorporate words beginning with each letter into our daily conversations. In other words, she focused on achieving a series of short-term goals to eventually reach her long-term goal of teaching her children to read and improving our vocabulary.

Set achievable short-term goals without losing sight of your long-term plans. More importantly, have fun meeting them!

As we grew older and our attention spans lengthened considerably, our parents were able to introduce more substantial short- as well as long-term goals. In grade school, our short-term goals centered on completing homework assignments in a timely fashion. In middle school, our parents involved us in evaluating our performances in various subjects on a weekly, monthly, and quarterly basis. By evaluating our performances regularly, our parents sought to foster our talents in subjects in which we excelled while identifying and improving areas of weakness.

Our parents believed it was never too early to start thinking ahead and creating long-term goals. As soon as we hit middle school, our parents encouraged us to think hard about what professions we might be interested in and what colleges we hoped to attend. You might think this ridiculous, as very few middle schoolers are aware of their talents and options at the time. Rest assured, our parents never expected our goals to remain unchanged (if that were true, Jane would be a professional ice skater now, and Soo would have graduated from Duke University!). Rather, our parents were simply interested in teaching us the process of thinking ahead and preparing for the future. Practice makes perfect for all things, and formulating and achieving long-term goals was no exception.

By the time we were teenagers, we recognized the importance and value of setting and attaining long-term goals. And this was no easy task for our parents, who realized quickly that simply reminding their children from time to time to attend college and get a rewarding job would not be good enough. Without first acquiring the skills necessary to set short- and long-term goals and follow through with them, no child will be able to buckle down for more than a decade to gain acceptance into a top college.

So, how do parents get kids to want to create goals for themselves? As we discussed before, it starts with instilling a healthy respect for delayed gratification. Furthermore, the ability to set and pursue both short- and long-term goals requires considerable perseverance and attention to detail, traits many Asians are well-known for.

If you ask Asian immigrants in this country how they managed to survive financially without welfare or financial assistance, despite significant language barriers and poverty, they will smile and tell you that their indomitable work ethic, perseverance, and attention to detail got them through the rough times. If you ask these same immigrants how they managed to raise children who surpassed others in the classroom despite the same obstacles, they will tell you the same thing.

Not that Asians alone should be singled out and praised—all immigrants, regardless of race, seem to hold these attributes very dear to their heart. It goes without saying that many immigrants left their native countries in hopes for a better life in America. Whether they left for the chance to receive an unparalleled education or to experience financial or personal freedom, the fact remains that despite the hardships they would face in a foreign country, these immigrants believed the potential advantages of coming to America far exceeded the disadvantages.

Asian immigrants came to this country and were given no breaks—they had to work for their future, and they were thrilled to even be given the chance to do so. They gladly took the jobs and worked the hours nobody wanted, and slowly distinguished themselves with high-quality work and a level of dedication to their jobs that was uncommon among the financially and socioeconomically challenged. Many of these Asian immigrants didn't call in sick, show up to work late, or perform poorly on the job. Rather, they went above and beyond what their minimum-wage jobs required, so much so that Asian immigrants are now considered by many to be among the most dependable and sought-after employees. Suffice it to say that what Asian immigrants lacked in financial security and language skills, they more than made up with their dedication to hard work, perseverance, and attention to detail.

Adopt a strong work ethic and an attitude of perserverance and attention to detail that your child can emulate.

As you might expect, this strong work ethic and perseverance has everything to do with setting and achieving both short- and long-term goals. First, help your child set goals that are attainable. In the beginning, it doesn't matter how small or trivial they are—setting goals that are impossible to reach will only discourage your child from trying the next time. For example, a goal for your toddler might be to learn to count to twenty; a goal for a grade school student might be to learn all the state capitals; an older child's goal might be to learn the basics of a foreign language. No matter what the goal, demand excellence in the end result. The key here is also to get your child involved in creating the goal: children who play an active role in the process will be more committed to the end result. When you help your child set and achieve a series of short-term goals, you instill the values of effort and perseverance.

What about attention to detail? The steps toward both short- and long-term goals should be clearly outlined and emphasized. For example, if you and your child's long-term goal is to get him accepted to College X, the numerous steps required to achieve this goal should be clearly delineated. These steps include meeting with a guidance counselor early in high school to discuss college plans, hand-selecting a challenging curriculum that will showcase your child's talents and improve his grade point average, and preparing for the SAT; later, visiting the college campus, filling out the application, and working on a personal statement. Remember: very few runners faced with completing a 10-mile marathon will find the finish line without breaking up the daunting task into smaller "hurdles." Strategies to finish the first few miles will drastically differ from methods employed to complete the middle and last legs of the marathon, and breaking down the journey into separate steps will certainly make completing the race successfully more feasible.

Actively involve your child in the development of his short- and long-term goals. Have him write down all his goals in a "goal notebook." This will increase his sense of accountability and thus his chance of succeeding.

Last but not least, there are very few goals that can be accomplished without considerable encouragement and accountability. It is essential that children, who often don't have the insight or experience to know how their current actions may impact their future, are carefully nurtured and monitored. Even the most carefully thought-out and well-crafted long-term goals will fall be the wayside without frequent parental guidance. Check in with your kids often. Talk to them to about how their goals are changing. Despite the resistance you may be met with, monitoring their goal-setting abilities is crucial to their success and to your peace of mind.

Parents can begin working on both short- and long-term goals early in their child's life. Despite the child's short attention span, parents can succeed if they construct reasonable goals compatible with their child's strengths and weaknesses, and if they keep the big picture in mind at all times. As your child grows older, getting him involved in the goal-forming process to increase accountability, providing encouragement, and clearly defining the steps to achieving the goals will ensure maximum academic success.

Secret 8: To-Do List

- **Set achievable short-term goals without losing sight of the long-term plans, and have fun meeting them!**
- **Adopt a strong work ethic and an attitude of perseverance and attention to detail that your child can emulate.**
- **Actively involve your child in the development of his short- and long-term goals. Have him write down his goals in a "goal notebook." This will increase his sense of accountability and thus his chance of succeeding.**

Secret 9

Teach Your Child the Art of Valuing Academic Success Over Social Status or Popularity

> **"In my opinion, Asians tend to succeed in the classroom because education is highly valued in Asian culture. In Korea, being an educator is a highly respected and well-paid profession. My parents instilled the value of education in me, and encouraged me to take it seriously, get good grades, and do my absolute best in school. Being good in school was fun, and it contributed to my self-esteem."**
>
> **—Suzanne Whang, award-winning stand-up comedian and host of *House Hunters*; graduate of Yale and Brown Universities**

The amount of schooling people pursue varies greatly, but what one chooses to accomplish during those years will have lifelong consequences. If you ask adults what their favorite memories of school are, you will be barraged with images of sleepovers, dances, football games, and parties. Women will speak of their prom dresses and high school sweethearts, while men will reminisce about victorious sports games and the good-looking girls they dated. On the flip side, you would be hard-pressed to find anyone who would speak fondly of school projects, standardized tests, or the college admission process.

Despite students' wishes, school is much more than a time to kick back, go to parties, and attend football games. One's academic performance during middle and high school can often determine the college one attends, if any at all. In turn, the college one attends can significantly influence the direction one's career takes.

Which is why we are surprised that the elementary, middle, and high school experience has yet to change significantly over the decades, despite how much more competitive the college admission process has become. Students still shower the football players, homecoming queens, and cheerleaders with undue respect and adulation while the students at the top of the class are often labeled as "teacher's pets" or "brown-nosers."

Although there are exceptions, the American school experience is rather uniform across the country. The goal is to be popular and well liked—if students can do that while still doing well in school, more power to them. But if they have to choose between being popular and underperforming, or doing well in school and being less popular, most kids will gladly see their grades drop.

For example, although high school is only a mere four years of our lifetime (the average life expectancy in America is now 80 for women, 76 for men, and is expected to increase), it's a crucial four years. When your child interviews for a competitive position, it will be her academic performance during high school (and college and graduate school) that is scrutinized, not her popularity. It will make no difference to a top executive in a prominent firm that your child was homecoming queen during high school; on the other hand, her performance in high school (and college and graduate school) will single her out.

Although even we revered the popular kids, our perspective changed considerably as we got older. It's inevitable that people are always going to admire those who are attractive, outgoing, and confident. Yet people in their twenties tend to admire those who are educated and doing well professionally more than those who can throw a football, no matter how good they look in a uniform. Adults in their thirties and forties tend to admire those with nice homes and successful careers. In our fifties and sixties, we admire those who have saved enough to put their children through college and retire early. In other words, what seemed so important in high school and middle school really does fade into the past.

The choices children make in school will impact the rest of their lives. We're not saying that you can't be popular, athletic, and a top student—we know many students who are. But we also know too many students who allowed their grades to fall by the wayside due to pressure to be well liked or popular. Peer pressure to conform to the American ideal is considerable and can even be overwhelming for many children. Knowing this, we do not blame the many teenagers who gambled with their education and future and lost. We blame the system.

In Asia, popularity is largely based on school performance. By and large, the top students tend to be the most popular and well liked. Many schools in Asia are still segregated based on gender and enforce a strict school-uniform code in order to minimize distraction for their students. Although Asia is now becoming more westernized, with many coed schools popping up in the more urban areas, school is still very much a place to sharpen one's mind, not flirt with the opposite sex or be seen in the latest fashion. Although this is also true in some America schools, for the most part, school is much more of a social event here than in Asia.

Learn to view intellect and personality as more effective builders of self-esteem than popularity or social status. This will stress the importance of academic achievement to your child.

With fewer distractions from the main purpose of school, students in Asian countries simply find it easier to focus on learning. Children will be children, of course, and cliques are universal in any setting where very diverse groups of people are thrown together. By no means are we saying that Asian classrooms are devoid of cliques—it is only natural for students to be drawn to the more attractive or magnetic members of the class. The difference lies in the importance placed on academic achievement and schooling. In Asia, children learn from an early age that those who perform well in school are to be admired. In America, the most popular students are typically revered for something other than their school performance. Sure, there are plenty of students who excel academically who are also attractive and good at a sport, but there's no question that it is not only their grades that are making them so well liked.

So what's a parent in America to do? Surely you can't change centuries of school customs overnight, and we wouldn't even want anyone to try. There are many traditions that are fun and highly memorable in the American school experience, and your children should enjoy them. On the other hand, there are many things you *can* do to ensure that your child makes being a good student more of a priority than being voted onto Homecoming Court.

As you might have guessed by now, it all starts in the home. We've all seen the TV movies of former homecoming queens who dressed their little girls in fancy clothing and enrolled them in beauty pageants in hopes that one day their daughters would earn the coveted Homecoming or Miss America crown. Then there are the stories of overzealous mothers who wanted so much for their daughters to become cheerleaders that they physically threatened or harmed others who stood in their way. It's especially important that families help their daughters develop healthy senses of self-esteem at an early age. Today, girls have to deal with complicated body-image issues. Get a head start by making sure your daughter feels valued because of her personality and intellect. This can be accomplished by praising scholastic efforts and achievements while downplaying social triumphs.

There are plenty of men who are guilty of similar grievances. There are countless former football players who, from the minute their sons could walk, made football an integral part of their lives. These fanatic fathers forced their sons to live and breathe the sport in hopes of playing college or professional ball, only to become irate or irrationally disappointed when their sons either showed little interest in the game or didn't make the cut.

It is only natural and healthy for parents to want their children to be well liked and surrounded by loyal friends. On the other hand, parents should not push their children to aim to be the most popular kids in school. In today's American schools, being popular typically entails little more than being good-looking, wearing the right clothes, having the right friends, or driving the right car. One's level of wealth or social status (or one's parents' wealth) also plays a large role in popularity, as does membership in elite groups such as sports teams. Instead, focus on cultivating a respect for academically oriented achievements.

Celebrating your child's academic achievements more than his social or sports-related triumphs will discourage him from clinging to measures of social status at school.

Celebrate your child's academics sucesses as much (if not more than) his social and sports-related triumphs (more about this in the next chapter). Stress the fact that, in the working world, those with a strong work ethic, impeccable moral character, and good personality are the most well liked, respected, and popular. Among adults in their twenties and thirties, the financially secure and professionally driven individuals are the ones who are respected and admired. We were certainly not the most popular kids at our high schools—we never had legions of boys calling our house, wore crowns on our heads, or got invitations to the elite drinking parties. Yet we think we turned out pretty well.

Kids nowadays are faced with huge amounts of stress and peer pressure. As a parent, you must at the same time give them freedom to experiment and guide them to success. Don't argue with your kids about relatively unimportant things like hairstyle, clothing, and the state of their room—become their ally during this stressful and difficult time period. Don't pressure them into running for homecoming queen or trying out for the football team—help them find and encourage them to excel in the extracurricular activities they enjoy. That said, don't forget that you set the rules around the house: make the priviledge of spending nights partying with friends dependent on school and standardized test performances. Never underestimate what a powerful influence you have in your kids' lives, despite what they tell you on a daily basis. As parents, you have the ability to influence how your children prioritize their grades, SATs, college preparation, and social life during high school. And as we alluded to before, the effort you make over the years can make a world of difference.

Although your child's social life should take the back burner, don't totally ignore its importance. Encourage your child to forge meaningful friendships with like-minded peers. Planning one social activity each weekend should keep your child refreshed and focused on academics during the week. Remember, be flexible: if your child's grades fall, schedule more time for schoolwork; if his grades are stellar, allow him more time to hang out with friends.

We understand that dealing with teenagers might be the hardest thing a parent has to do. Our parents certainly struggled with Jane—your typical American high school kid who wanted to spend as much time as humanly possible talking on the phone and hanging out with her friends. Although she understood the importance of doing well, she had witnessed her older sister breeze through high school and obtain a scholarship to the university of her choice. Because Soo had made it look relatively easy, Jane assumed she could balance her schoolwork and social life with little difficulty.

Prior to Jane's freshman year of high school, our family moved from the States to Tokyo, where our parents had accepted demanding jobs with Nortel Networks and IBM. During the first few months of Jane's freshman year, our parents woke up early and came home late, leaving little time or energy to supervise Jane and her schoolwork. Although Jane knew that her parents' top priority had always been helping their daughter get a solid education and gain admission to a top college, at the time they seemed much more preoccupied with their own careers than her education. And as their priorities temporarily shifted, so did Jane's.

For the first time ever, Jane found herself with more freedom than she knew what to do with. Although freedom is a wonderful thing when one is mature enough to make educated decisions, we hope you'll agree with us that the vast majority of high school students lack this maturity. Jane certainly didn't possess it—before long, she started spending more time with her friends after school. Rather than studying and doing her homework, she went shopping, hung out in music stores and video arcades, and gossiped with her friends in coffee shops. Although Jane was aware she was falling behind in certain classes, her social life had become her top priority.

Her happiness and newfound popularity, however, were short-lived. After a semester of nonstop partying and minimal studying, Jane brought home a report card that contained two letter grades our parents had never seen before—two C's. Realizing that their hectic schedules and relative absence from the home were largely responsible, both our parents vowed to make it home in time for dinner and resume their roles as educators (they had become fatigued couch potatoes). They also set strict ground rules that involved Jane coming home directly after school on days she was not involved with the tennis team and calling our mother at work to "check in." Jane was to post a class syllabus on the refrigerator and a calendar outlining test dates so that our parents could monitor her progress. Jane's hour- to two-hour-long telephone conversations at night that our parents had largely ignored also came to a screeching halt—she was no longer allowed to talk on the phone for more than a total of twenty minutes on a school night.

Although our parents were dedicated and determined for Jane to improve her grades in those areas she was having difficulty with, we believe the manner in which they handled it was key. First, they discussed with her that they were not satisfied with her grades and believed she could do better. They talked about the reasons why Jane felt her grades in certain subjects were lower than others and what strategies she could employ to improve them. After Jane and our parents discussed and agreed upon a "plan of attack," our parents put some guidelines in place. Although they were more than willing and happy for Jane to start the plan of attack on her own, they made it very clear that certain things were going to have to change. For starters, our parents would monitor her activities outside of school and drastically reduce the amount of unsupervised free time she had grown accustomed to. They set parameters for Jane's grades to improve; however, they gave her some latitude to try and raise her grades on her own without extensive parental involvement. As this example highlights, a give-and-take approach works far better with teenagers than a completely dictatorial tone.

Stay on top of your child's progress in school by keeping a "grade log" according to subject. This is a great way to keep track of improvements or spot downward trends early on.

In the beginning, suffice it to say Jane felt like a prisoner in her own home, with our parents being her parole officers. Gone were the carefree afternoons listening to music at Tower Records—her afternoons and evenings were now dedicated to math and science. Our parents also enforced the twenty-minute telephone rule like top-security prison wardens.

Jane now laughingly recalls an evening when she found out just how serious our parents were about the new rules. One evening after Jane had already chatted on the phone for twenty minutes, her friend Justin called. Disregarding the rule, Jane picked up the phone and talked for an additional fifteen minutes. Although our father was aware of the breach, he chose to give Jane the benefit of the doubt and decided to wait to see if it happened again. The next evening, another of Jane's friends called after her twenty minutes had already been used. When our father saw Jane casually reach for the phone, he sprang into action and answered the phone before her. After telling the caller that Jane was unavailable, he proceeded to tell the caller to "call back during spring break." Needless to say, Jane was mortified. After all, it was January, and spring break was months away!

Jane did eventually cool down, and soon enough she got back on track. Her grades improved considerably the next semester, after which she was able to speak on the phone between thirty and forty-five minutes a night. Years later, Jane realizes how grateful she is that our parents helped her achieve her best during high school. She cringes when she thinks about where she might be if our parents hadn't intervened when they did—after all, all the popularity in the world during school doesn't bring you personal, financial, or professional happiness as an adult if you don't use those years to obtain a first-rate education.

School performance is relative, so many of you may be thinking "Two C's? I would be *happy* if my child brought home a report card with two C's!" Every parent has different expectations for their children—we recognize that one parent's "C" might be another parent's "A." Although Jane was not a star student like her sister, she was by no means a bad student. With the proper guidance and measures in place, she was an above-average student. Without it, she was an average student. It was that simple.

Middle and high school, for most kids, is an angst-ridden time. Your children are worrying about how to avoid acne, who to take to the next school dance, and what to wear to school. Although kids are notoriously hard to talk to, a few words of encouragement and sympathy can go a long way. This *is* a tough time for most, and parents can score big with their unruly children by sitting down and talking about that fact, before stressing the importance of excelling academically.

Let's face it: there are only a handful of kids who can be consoled by prospects of an Ivy League college education and a bright professional future when faced with much more urgent, immediately traumatizing matters—no matter how silly they might find the dilemma later on. As parents, you'll find the key to handling these years with all its angst is to acknowledge the difficulty of the situation without belittling or exaggerating its significance.

If at all possible, parents can also make their job easier by choosing their child's high school carefully. It goes without saying that not all schools are created equal—chances are schools in Beverly Hills are far more image-conscious than private, same-sex schools in the Northeast that require uniforms. Parents who want their children to be in an environment that fosters learning and preparation for college and the future will choose their child's schools judiciously. Kids will be kids, after all; had Soo attended the local high school—where far fewer graduates attended four-year colleges and where being seen in the latest fashion was all the rage—rather than the North Carolina School of Science and Mathematics, who knows if her talents in science and math would have been nurtured to the degree that they were.

Research is the key. Parents should gather as much information as they can on the school they are contemplating sending their children to. This requires frequent visits to the school as well as discussions, meetings, and telephone calls with other parents, students, and guidance counselors. First and foremost, parents need to be comfortable with the school's track record. If your child is seeking entrance into a top-tier college, research what percentage of students attended four-year universities and what schools they attended for each high school you are considering.

The atmosphere (or ambience) of the school is important to assess as well—you will want to get a keen sense that education, not extracurricular activities or social events, are the school's top priority. You should get this sense from speaking with students, parents, and educators at the school. Always remember that while you are there everyone is putting on their best face—if your gut instinct is telling you that the school is not what you are looking for, you are probably right.

As parents, you may sympathize with your children when they experience rejection or behave a certain way to gain popularity among their peers, but never indulge their fears. Despite your own high school experiences or beliefs, never let them see that you also are overly concerned with their popularity or image in high school. Your main concern should be your children's grades and college aspirations.

This chapter is so important it deserves a brief summary. To your children, "success" in school requires wearing the right clothes, having the right friends, or dating the best-looking people. Your mission is to teach and convince them to value learning by performing well in school and establishing a solid academic base on which they can build their future. Encouraging them to hang out and befriend similarly minded peers despite popularity (or lack thereof) should also strengthen their commitment to academic excellence.

It may seem like an uphill battle, but your efforts will not go unrewarded. Years down the road, your children will only remotely remember how popular they were in high school. On the other hand, they'll be able to see how where they went to college and what they did there has shaped their lives.

Secret 9: To-Do List

- Learn to view intellect and personality as far more effective builders of self-esteem than popularity or social status. This will stress the importance of academic achievement to your child.

- Celebrating your child's academic achievements more than his social or sports-related triumphs will discourage him from clinging to measures of social status at school.

- Although your child's social life should take the back burner to his schoolwork, don't totally ignore its importance. Encourage your child to forge meaningful friendships with like-minded peers. Planning one social activity each weekend should keep your child refreshed and focused on academics during the week. Remember to be flexible: if your child's grades fall, schedule more time for schoolwork; if his grades are stellar, allow him more time to hang out with his friends.

- Stay on top of your child's progress in school by keeping a "grade log" according to school subject. This log is a great way to spot downward trends early and keep track of improvements.

Secret 10

Reward Positive School Performances and Devise a Plan of Attack for Poor School Performances

> **"My parents never tried to 'boost' my ego with undeserved praise. If anything, they took pains to always point out the many ways I could improve. While American parents continually try to reinforce their child's self-esteem, my parents did quite the opposite! But that very sense of insecurity, instilled in me by my perfectionist parents, is probably what drove me to achieve as much as I have."**
>
> **—Tess Gerritsen, best-selling physician-author of *The Surgeon***

In the previous chapter, we talked about how parents can help kids learn to value academic success over popularity. Now we're going to reveal to you the single most powerful weapon you, as a parent, can use to make this goal a reality: positive reinforcement and reward.

All parents and educators feel strongly that positive reinforcement works and that stellar performances in school should be rewarded. On the other hand, many American parents also reward their children for mediocre school performances, fearing that if they are too negative, they might discourage their children into bringing home even poorer grades. On the flip side, some Asian parents tend to enforce negative consequences or harsh punishment for bad grades. Although this tactic may improve school performance in children short-term, the resentment and fear this strategy often fosters may prevent these children from associating learning and education with fun, freedom, and power. Neither rewarding your children unnecessarily nor punishing them excessively is the best approach to improving their school performance—the answer lies somewhere in the middle.

Let's start with the concept that most parents have no problem accepting—the concept that positive reinforcement works, and works well. It goes without saying that actions that are rewarded will be repeated. Children want very much to please their parents, despite what many of them say. Often, a parent's praise or happiness will be positive reinforcement enough for many children to continue desired behaviors. A girl who is told by her parents that she is good at math will continue to seek ways to prove that mom and dad are right; a boy who begins to receive compliments from his father will suddenly no longer find football practice a chore.

Positive reinforcement works by building confidence and self-esteem—children who are praised by their parents or are rewarded for effective performances develop confidence that often leads to even greater achievement and happiness. Children who are constantly put down or discouraged rarely develop the confidence to succeed—these children see their parents' disapproving glares or disappointed expressions and learn that they can do nothing right.

Having spent a considerable amount of time with her five-year-old niece, Soo has witnessed the power of positive reinforcement firsthand. Leila, a delightful five-year-old who loves to watch videos, play with Barbie, and torture her younger brother, is Soo's niece by marriage. When Leila was younger, Soo and her husband, Joe, would spend much of their time with Leila playing board games or watching cartoons on the Disney Channel or Nickelodeon. As Leila grew older and entered pre-school, however, Soo wanted to add an educational slant to their activities.

Shortly after Leila's fourth birthday, Soo invented the game Leila would later nickname "Five Words." As you might have guessed, the concept of the game was quite simple. Thanks to her father who owned and ran a computer business, Leila had developed a love for the computer early on (she had mastered how to control a mouse before she was three!). The first thing Leila insisted on doing whenever she visited Soo was surf the Internet for trailers of her favorite Disney movies and video games featuring her favorite cartoon character, Kim Possible.

Soo invented the game "Five Words" just as Leila was learning to read and write. While scanning the Internet for fun games and trailers, she would pick out five simple words to teach Leila. After copying the words onto a Microsoft Word document and enlarging them on the screen, Leila would rehearse the words with Soo until she was able to read all five of them without help. When she was finished, Soo would print out the five words on a colorful piece of paper and present it to Leila as a cherished "gift." Leila would later show this paper to her parents and grandparents while bragging that she had learned yet another five words of the English language.

To make a long story short, Leila began to look forward to playing the game "Five Words" with Soo. Soon enough, Leila wanted to play the game more than she wanted to watch *Finding Nemo* for the fiftieth time or play Barbie. The positive reinforcement Soo and the game had provided Leila was twofold. On the one hand, Leila's successful mastery of the five words resulted in lavish amounts of praise from other family members. On the other hand, the game allowed Leila to experience the joy of learning firsthand. The pride and joy on her face after she mastered how to read those five words was unmistakable to Soo. The young girl reaped both the internal (self-satisfaction) and external (praise and admiration from outsiders) rewards of learning.

The majority of Americans today believe in the power of positive reinforcement and are quick to praise their children every chance they get. There is the hidden fear in every loving family that not doing so will result in a discouraged or unhappy child who will inevitably grow up to be an unhappy, maladjusted adult. To avoid this, parents heap praise on their children after every activity, every game, and every lesson—regardless of performance.

And why not always sing your child's praises, regardless of how well he or she performs? Why not praise the effort, regardless of outcome? If a child studies hard and brings home a report card full of C's, why not act as happy as if he had brought home straight A's?

Stress effort first and foremost, but don't forget about the importance of achievement!

American parents believe that getting in the race and putting forth one's best effort is what is important, regardless of whether one wins or loses. As Americans, we agree with this belief—it is certainly better to try and fail than not to try at all. On the other hand, Asian parents tend to stress the importance of both getting in the race, trying your hardest, *and* winning it, and this makes all the difference. They believe in adopting the attitude that both entering and excelling in the race are important. The simple example of a two-year-old learning his ABC's (an experience that all parents have) nicely illustrates the different mindsets. Many parents can recall encouraging their child to recite the alphabet, clapping their hands at every correct letter with absolute glee while glossing over the mistakes. Asian parents take the theory of positive reinforcement one step further—like other parents, they too praise their child just for getting in the race (attempting to recite the alphabet). On the other hand, they further reward their child for winning the race (correctly reciting the alphabet). Despite what some people believe, it is possible to reward your child for trying to recite the alphabet correctly but also let him know that he did not get it right without permanently damaging his self-esteem. There is, after all, a right and a wrong way of reciting the alphabet, and parents can praise their child's efforts yet encourage him to try again and "get it right." For example, if your child does a good job of reciting the alphabet but continues to reverse the order of a few letters, try saying something along the lines of, "You did a great job! Can we review a couple of the letters that you are having difficulty with? Let me go over it first, and then you can try." This approach allows you to offer praise for a job well done while acknowledging your child's mistakes and demonstrating the correct way to perform the task. You also will encourage him to continue to try until he has mastered it. The key lies in not discouraging a child for his mistakes, and making it clear that a correct answer is within his grasp. Imagine how happy the child will be when he does it right all on his own!

Think of putting the concept of positive reinforcement on a sliding scale. Parents on one extreme are quick to offer harsh criticism every time their child fails to meet their expectations. We all know parents who fall into this category, and although there are certainly some success stories, the negative psychological repercussions are usually far more destructive than any short-term academic or educational gains.

Parents on the other extreme believe in positively reinforcing their child's every success and failure, however small or large. While these parents develop healthy relationships with their children based on respect and love, they are also unknowingly doing their child a disservice. While their continual and constant praise serves to enable their children to develop healthy self-esteem and high confidence levels, the lack of parental direction can leave these children unfocused and confused as to where their real talents and interests lie. If after three years of hacking away at the piano, your son still sounds as terrible as he did the first day, don't gush about how much he's improved. Maybe it's time for him to try something new. The same theory applies to pursuing a certain career path (this will be discussed in depth in the next chapter). If your son is hell-bent on becoming a math professor but can barely pass geometry despite having put his best foot forward, giving him undeserved praise and advocating that he "stick it out" may not be the best solution. As a parent, you can still offer emotional support by acknowledging that you admire his perseverance. However, when asked if he should continue to pursue his dream, you may need to suggest a more realistic alternative that is in line with his strengths and personality.

Try to place yourself in the middle of the scale. Praise your child for a job well done. On the other hand, reserve your best and most effusive praise for his or her biggest accomplishments, and don't be too quick to applaud him or her for less than stellar performances. Congratulate your son's B+ on his algebra test but point out the silly mental mistakes that could have given him an A! Encourage your child to tackle every educational milestone with gusto but also teach him to expect the best results possible. Show your child that you can be proud of his efforts yet disappointed with his performance. You'll be amazed how much more he'll want to achieve the next time around.

It's okay to show your child that you are proud of his effort yet unsatisfied with his performance. Undeserved praise will only do your child a disservice.

There are few things more destructive to a child's educational development and scholastic achievement than a parent who denies their child praise or positive reinforcement (Asian parents, of course, can also fall into this category, which we will touch upon at the end of the book). However, parents who offer constant praise toward all of their child's successes and failures are ultimately doing their child a disservice. The best thing to do is to employ positive reinforcement when warranted while also teaching your child to recognize his mistakes. When your child fails to meet his potential, actively devise a plan of attack. You'll bring out the best in your child in the classroom while maintaining his self-confidence and enthusiasm to tackle the next assignment, however big or small.

Secret 10: To-Do List

- **Stress effort first and foremost, but don't forget about the importance of achievement!**
- **Be realistic with your child about his abilities and talents.**
- **It is okay to show your child that you are proud of his effort yet unsatisfied with his performance. Undeserved praise will only do your child a disservice.**

Secret 11

Forget the "Do Whatever Makes You Happy" Mentality and Strive for Professions with Financial Security and Intellectual Fulfillment

Being a parent is perhaps the most difficult job in the world. No other job or profession demands as much emotional and physical investment and sacrifice. While most professionals train for years after high school in order to prepare for their jobs (surgeons train for at least thirteen years after high school before they are allowed to operate), new parents get *no* training prior to embarking on the most important journey and job of their lives. Despite their relative lack of training, however, parents are expected to raise healthy, happy, well-adjusted, and self-motivated children who will eventually become happy, healthy, well-adjusted, and self-motivated contributing members of society.

Most parents will agree it's well worth the effort, though: there is no greater feeling than seeing your guidance produce positive results in your child's life. So how does one learn to become a parent who encourages and guides a child in the right direction?

It goes without saying that first and foremost all parents want their child to be healthy and happy. You'd certainly be hard-pressed to find any parent who would prefer academic excellence and achievement to personal fulfillment and happiness for their child. Even the most ambitious of parents, we dare say, would prefer their child to be a happy and fulfilled supermarket cashier than a despondent CEO of a Fortune 500 company.

We often hear parents tell their children, "We just want you to be happy!" and perhaps no other statement parents make rings truer. The love parents possess for their children is selfless and all-consuming. However, it's important not to forget that you are the adults in the family with years of experience under your belt. What your children believe will make them happy may differ significantly from what you think will fulfill them in the long run.

For parents, it is important to learn that wanting your child to be happy and wanting the best for him when it comes to his future career are not mutually exclusive. There are parents who feel that any guidance or direction they give may undermine their child's happiness, or be misconstrued as being overbearing or pushy. Needless to say, many children with parents who fall into this category do not achieve their full potential. And although they may have had a more carefree or fun-filled childhood, the happiness that comes from achieving greatness on a personal and professional level (the kind that can only come with considerable encouragement and guidance) may elude them for the rest of their adult lives.

Parents at the other end of the spectrum place too little importance on their child's happiness and are of the mindset that a child is in no position to know what will make him or her happy. These parents firmly believe they are doing their children a disservice if they do not direct them (at times forcefully) down a certain career path. These parents often have just as good intentions as the parents discussed previously; they truly feel that what they think is best for their children will eventually make them happy. Unfortunately, their children are likely to be no happier or more professionally successful than their peers. Having experienced heavy parental pressure throughout much of their childhood, these children will tend to rebel during their adolescent or young adult years. In doing so, their first instinct will be to stray from the path chosen for them by their parents—a path that usually involves attending college and pursuing a financially secure career.

Don't be afraid to voice your opinions regarding your child's career choices. What your child thinks will make him happy now may differ significantly from what you believe will fulfill him in the long run. Strike a balance between maintaining his happiness and guiding him in the right direction.

Although there are many jobs that provide personal fulfillment and financial security, certain professions provide more financial security than others. According to the U.S. Department of Labor, the highest paid U.S. employees belong to only a handful of professionals. Physicians of various specialties (with surgeons and obstetricians leading the pack) make up seven of the top ten highest paid professionals; lawyers are twelfth on the list, judges nineteenth. Other professionals that made it into the top twenty include chief executives, as well as computer and information systems managers and various specialty engineers.

If you think carefully about the professions we just mentioned, you will see that these jobs have more in common than just financial security or wealth—many of the above-mentioned professions are considered among the most intellectually stimulating and rewarding in the world. What these top-paid professions also have in common is the high level of education required to get the job done—suffice it to say, no high school diploma will secure you a position as a physician, lawyer, engineer, or executive.

Although there are many reasons why parents should encourage their children to pursue fields that are both intellectually stimulating and financially rewarding, there is only one big reason *not* to pursue these professions: the rather lengthy and rigorous amount of schooling involved. Looking back, Soo spent every third night in the hospital during her twenties while many of her peers were living the high life and partying. Jane spent months preparing for the Pennsylvania Bar (times two!) while her peers went to one social event after another. We were able to do that because we had an appreciation and love for learning given to us by our parents—and an understanding that education leads to professional security. Savvy parents who want their children to achieve the happiness and fulfillment an intellectually stimulating and financially secure position provides know how to raise their children to view the many years of education required to secure a professional job as well worth their time.

Talk early and often with your child about his career choices. As he gets older, schedule one-on-one meetings with him and between him and his educators and other mentors. Emphasize professions with financial security and intellectual fulfillment.

However well intentioned they may be, parents sometimes underestimate the importance of financial stability or security in their child's future happiness. We know many parents who tell their children that all they care about is their happiness, regardless of how much money they make or what profession they choose. This mistake is a common one and stems from the notion that one does not need financial security in order to be happy. While it is true that you don't need to be rich to be happy, we know very few people who are unable to pay their bills and are satisfied with life.

Certainly no one should ever underestimate the satisfaction and happiness financial security can provide—struggling to put food on the table and pay one's bills can be a considerable psychological and emotional burden for any man or woman (so much so that money differences and finances are cited as the number one cause of divorce in America today!). The fact of the matter is, financial security provided by a well-paid job can put your mind at ease and allow you and your family to concentrate on other, more enjoyable, things. And it's true a dozen degrees won't necessarily guarantee you wealth. But—and this is an important but—higher education *combined* with financial security can work wonders. In fact, we believe the two are intimately connected—that education is a more reliable and proven road to wealth, intellectual freedom, and social enlightenment. Think of all the individuals one meets and of all the opportunities presented to a person in college or graduate school. It may not happen over night, but a legal career can set the foundation for starting your own business, becoming a professor, or writing a book. Education is never a waste—it not only opens doors, but also greatly increases your chances for financial security by providing you with skills the average person does not have.

So, how exactly do parents make this connection in their children's minds? Even our parents—whose own lives were a model of the importance of education—had trouble guiding their daughters along the same path. Although Soo knew she wanted to pursue medicine from an early age, Jane was far more uncertain about going to law school. One year shy of college graduation, it was clear that Jane, who was about to graduate with a degree in international studies, still had no set plans for the future. She did, however, know what she loved to do and what she was good at—she loved writing, learning new languages and cultures, and working with disadvantaged people. Still, our parents started to panic. They began pestering Jane about her future plans. Irritated, Jane would often curtly reply that she would pursue a career in writing and make ends meet by writing or editing for a magazine.

Unimpressed by Jane's future plans, our parents weighed her strengths, weaknesses, and personality, and decided that law school might provide their daughter with the financial security that other jobs might not. After they made it clear that they would not financially support her after college, Jane soon realized that she was not going to make ends meet without an alternate plan. Dragging her feet most of the way, Jane applied to several law schools and gained admission to a few.

Back then, Jane was full of resentment toward what she thought were our dictatorial parents. It seemed like she fought with them every other day. Accusing our parents of not caring about her happiness and wanting her to become wealthy just so that they could brag that they had a doctor and a lawyer in the family, Jane demanded that they leave her alone and let her be happy. Many of Jane's friends at the time had "cool" jobs working in bookstores, coffee shops, or restaurants. If *their* parents didn't seem to mind, why should hers?

The answer, quite simply, was that our parents were not like other parents. Much more interested in keeping their daughter's future best interest at heart than placating her for the time being, they stood firm in their belief that Jane should attend law school. Although Jane would have disagreed at the time, our parents knew she would not be happy unless she was both intellectually stimulated and financially secure. None of the professions Jane had proposed to our parents had a decent chance of guaranteeing both, and our parents were well aware that Jane was (and still is!) an individual who loved to travel, eat at ethnic restaurants, and see Broadway shows. How would she have the flexibility to do all the things she loved if she didn't earn a decent salary?

Not that we're saying that higher education naturally or automatically equates with a higher salary—in fact, we see images that contradict this on a daily basis. Every day on television we see singers, actors, and athletes who may not have even graduated from high school making millions of dollars a year. But as parents, you must teach your kids that wealthy high school dropouts are the exception rather than the rule. Contrary to what the media might have viewers believe, most high school or college dropouts that pursue their dreams in the entertainment industry achieve neither fame nor fortune. On the other hand, individuals who graduate from college and/or graduate school greatly increase their chances of landing jobs that are both intellectually fulfilling and financially rewarding.

To help determine the best career path for your child, evaluate what he enjoys, what he is good at, what challenges him, and what kind of lifestyle he sees for himself in the future. Make it clear that financially secure *and* intellectually fulfilled college dropouts are the exception rather than the rule!

Getting back to how Jane ultimately became a lawyer, we wish we could say that Jane was as thrilled about getting into law school as our parents. Convinced they were trying to control her life, Jane deferred law school for a year and made it her mission to prove to everyone that she could achieve both financial independence and the happiness that comes with job satisfaction without more education.

Determined to prove our parents wrong, Jane proceeded to hold down a series of jobs editing newsletters, waiting tables, and working as an office assistant in various companies. Months into what was supposed to be the best year of her life, Jane had already spent her savings and as a result, had to move in with Soo to make ends meet. Worse than being financially strapped, however, was the fact that the normally optimistic Jane was now unhappy and stressed out. She interviewed for two of her dream positions (one position with an advertising firm, the other with a trade-magazine publishing company) only to ultimately lose the position to candidates with graduate school degrees.

Shortly after being turned down for the second position, Jane decided she had had enough. Unsatisfied with her standard of living and now eager to open new professional doors by furthering her education, Jane enrolled in law school the following year. Although we can't say that the three years Jane endured at Temple Law School were all fun and games, we can say that she is happy and grateful for the stimulating and challenging career she has today. Years after she fought with our parents for trying to control her life by encouraging her to get her law degree, she now admits that our parents were right all along.

Finances aside, we'd like to remind you of the advantages that a rigorous education can provide. As we alluded to many times, education can provide an individual great joy if a love of learning is nurtured carefully. As far as life's greatest gifts go, love of learning ranks way up there—after all, it costs nothing, does not discriminate based on race and socioeconomic status, is attainable by all, and is the gift that keeps on giving.

One of our all-time favorite quotes comes from the hugely popular philanthropist and TV diva Oprah Winfrey. A great believer in education and the personal wealth and growth that it provides (mainly from personal experience), Oprah loves to say that "knowledge is power." According to Oprah, education frees the imprisoned mind, exposing a person to new cultures, beliefs, and regions of the world. Education also directly battles ignorance and fear, the two most powerful drivers of hate crimes and prejudice in the world.

Education also brings people of like mind and spirit together. In college, we truly believed we were bound together with men and women who, like us, wanted to make a difference in the world. As different as we were on an individual basis (race, socioeconomic status, culture), we all had the pursuit and love of higher education in common.

We have had the privilege, through attending college and graduate school, of receiving a top-notch education and acquiring skills that are unique and highly desired by the community and mankind. In the process of doing so, we have befriended countless men and women of different backgrounds and beliefs that challenged us and expanded our limited knowledge of the world we live in. This, more than any financial rewards our education has provided us, is perhaps education's greatest achievement.

Do your child a favor by being honest with them: teach them how much financial insecurity will affect their happiness in the long-run. Although an education certainly does not guarantee a high salary, no other means will consistently open as many doors on an intellectual, social, and financial level.

Secret 11: To-Do List

- Don't be afraid to voice your opinions regarding your child's career choices. What your child thinks will make him happy now may differ significantly from what you believe will fulfill him in the long run. Strike a balance between maintaining his happiness and guiding him in the right direction.
- Talk early and often with your child about his career choices. As he gets older, schedule one-on-one meetings with him and between him and his educators and other mentors. Emphasize professions with financial security and intellectual fulfillment.
- Teach your child never to underestimate the physical, emotional, and social havoc financial insecurity can wreak, even if one loves what he does for a living.
- To help determine the best career path for your child, evaluate what he enjoys, what he is good at, what challenges him, and what lifestyle he desires in the future.

Secret 12

Keep Your Money in Perspective

> **"Education and knowledge provides an individual with so many different kinds of wealth that the truly educated rarely feel the need to flaunt the material kind."**
>
> **—Soo Kim Abboud, M.D.**

As we discussed in the previous chapter, parents should encourage their children to pursue careers with financial security. However, you have to be careful not to make money their only incentive to succeed. Your children will never be truly fulfilled if all they're after is a big paycheck. On the flip side of the coin, parents who *are* wealthy have to be careful not to let the opposite happen: allow their kids to be lackadaisical in their academic pursuits because they have considerable financial security. It's a delicate balance to strike but one that is necessary for your child's ultimate happiness.

Certainly money can influence a child's career choice, particularly if he or she never had enough as a child. Soo remembers deciding very early on in her high school career that she would become a physician. She even recalls wanting to become a surgeon (although she didn't know what otolaryngology was back then) because she learned that they were the highest paid of the doctors. Although Soo was drawn to medicine because of her love and talent for science and biology, the financial security afforded by the medical profession (particularly in those days) was never far from her thoughts. As wonderful a childhood as our parents had afforded her, she didn't want to live paycheck to paycheck. She wanted to be able to afford a vacation more than once every three years, and she didn't want to keep going to the nearest beach. She dreamed of exotic travel destinations . . . Singapore, Thailand, and Greece, to name a few.

Our father worked as a computer programmer for much of his life and brought home an adequate but not abundant salary. Our mother, also trained to be a computer programmer, opted to stay home and raise her two daughters. Although our father was able to provide the essentials, we didn't have the luxury of cable television in our rooms, trendy clothing, or frequent meals at restaurants. We remember our mother spending countless hours clipping coupons and our father saving all his change in a glass jar at the end of each day. We remember getting a dollar a week for our allowance and lying to our friends that we received five dollars, which was closer to the average back then. Observing our parents fight to pay the bills and raise a family on a tight budget instilled in us a healthy respect for the hard-earned dollar. To this day, Jane will pick up a penny if she sees one lying on the street.

Our family's financial situation changed during Soo's freshman year at Johns Hopkins. Our father received an offer to head up a project for Nortel in Tokyo, Japan. He would be transferred for a period of two to three years. During that time, all his expenses in

Japan such as housing, food, and transportation would be paid through the company. The mortgage for our home in North Carolina would also be covered so that we could eventually return to it. Here's the kicker—our father's salary would more than triple!

We knew none of this until years later. Although our parents had come into a great deal of money, they acted and lived no differently than before. They still did not buy Jane the designer clothes she craved. Soo only received her coveted new car after she got accepted into medical school. And let us tell you something: the Toyota Tercel, although dependable, is by no means luxurious!

You may be thinking to yourself, "So what if Soo had gotten a nice sports car the same year her parents came into wealth? How would that have affected her down the road? I'm sure she still would have accomplished what she has today." And you may be right. It is quite possible that Soo's values may have been so deeply embedded by the time she attended college that a new car or extra cash might not have influenced her dedication to her classes . . . but they might have. She might have slacked off on her studies because she had extra cash to spend with her friends. If our parents had provided her with more money, she might not have been as motivated to earn it on her own.

So, do less wealthy parents have an advantage when it comes to motivating their children to succeed academically?

We think they do. It is easier to instill an appreciation for money and for financially rewarding professional careers in your child if they are not surrounded by too much money. We are not saying that being impoverished is a good thing for any child—*some* money is necessary to ensure a good education (books, educational activities, and sometimes the appropriate schooling all cost money). But the good news is, you don't need a lot of it in order to raise a child who is successful at school, in college, and eventually in the workplace.

It is important for parents to convey to their children that performing well in school increases their chances of future financial stability, which can impact their overall sense of well-being and happiness.

Of course, money-respecting children without a love of learning or respect for what education can add to one's life will not be successful in college or in their professional endeavors. As we said before, it is only when both a love for learning and respect for money are combined that children become self-sufficient and educated adults. Children who are taught to chase after the dollar but not to have a healthy respect for education and its value will never have the patience to complete the years of higher learning that college graduates and professionals must endure. Instead, they will fill their heads with dreams of striking it rich and ultimately suffer the consequences of ill-fated get-rich-quick schemes and scams.

So . . . what's a wealthy parent to do? It seems unfair to ask parents of considerable wealth amassed from years of hard work and sacrifice to live in a shack for the sake of their children's future. Rest assured, this is not what we're advising you to do. Parents who are well off should provide as many advantages and opportunities for their children as they can. After all, they have worked hard to ensure the best schooling and educational tools for their children, and we salute them. On the other hand, with considerable wealth comes an increased risk of lazy, unmotivated, and spoiled children.

If you are part of a modest-income family, encourage your child to pursue careers that offer both personal fulfillment and financial reward. Teach him that happiness is in some part dependent on financial stability.

Let us give you an example. A close friend of Soo's from college, who we will call "Dave," came from a well-to-do Chinese-American family. For a number of years Dave's parents had worked overseas, and by the time Dave was in college, they had amassed a great deal of wealth. Dave was able to attend college without paying a dime of his own money (Johns Hopkins is not a cheap university) and also was given a wide variety of credit cards for his expenses (which included movies, trips, dining at fancy restaurants, etc.).

Dave was a smart and gentle guy with a deep appreciation for education, which his parents had appropriately passed down to him. However, he no longer had the drive to work hard to ensure the brightest professional and financial future for himself. Worst-case scenario, he thought he could coast through college with marginal grades and still get into medical school. Even if he didn't make it into medical school, his parents had enough money to support him in the interim. Surely they would help him out should the unthinkable happen.

You can guess what happened to Dave, despite Soo's urging him throughout college to study harder and spend less money. Dave put in just enough effort to adequately complete his course load and earn his degree. And the unthinkable *did* happen: at the end of his senior year, every medical school had rejected him.

We wish we could say that Dave changed his attitude immediately afterward and started appreciating how much effort a professional career demanded. For three years after college, Dave held down a series of low-paying jobs while basically living off his parents' credit cards. It was not until his parents pulled the plug that he forced himself to take out a student loan and earn his master's degree. You see, because his parents had always provided for him, Dave had never internalized the need for financial security. They simply made it too easy for him. Today, Dave is a physician and is doing well.

If you are wealthy, provide your child with incentives to excel academically that are not financial in origin. These incentives may include (but are not limited to) increased self-esteem and family pride, a love of learning, a respect for higher education and the skills it imparts, and the satisfaction that comes from setting and achieving goals.

We mentioned earlier that extremely wealthy parents might be at increased risk of raising professionally unmotivated children. If you are wealthy, the key is to provide incentives to excel academically that are not financial in origin. Luckily, there are many incentives to achieving academic and professional success. They include family pride, love of learning, or respect for higher education, which we discussed in Secrets 1 and 2. The more incentives you can provide your children, the more likely they are to succeed.

A success story comes to mind involving one of Soo's closest college friends, a Chinese-American named Cathy. Cathy was the eldest daughter of two Chinese immigrant parents who had struck gold with their independent computer software development program while Cathy was only an infant. For as long as Cathy could remember, her parents were practically retired. Although they still dabbled in various computer projects, they no longer had to work full-time for income.

Although Cathy's parents had amassed considerable wealth, they wanted their daughter to appreciate the value of education and money. Cathy recalls living in a very nice but not luxurious home for much of her childhood. Despite her parents' desires to live large and travel frequently to exotic places, they lived modestly and limited their family vacations to once or twice a year. During these vacations they would stay in the nicest hotels, but they made it a point not to consistently surround their two daughters with all that wealth could buy. Soo recalls Cathy telling her that she never knew just how wealthy her parents were until she graduated college, when her parents offered to pay all of her student loans.

Make your child pay for some, if not all, of his or her college education. This will instill in him an appreciation for how hard a person has to work to make ends meet.

Because Cathy's parents knew that achieving financial security would be less of an issue for their two daughters, they aimed to provide their children with other incentives to perform well in school. Since both parents were home often, they chose to spend much of their time teaching their two daughters everything from reading and writing to Chinese, arithmetic, and piano. Because of the time their parents invested in them, both Cathy and her sister understood how important their education was to their parents and how important *they* were to their parents. Cathy recalls her parents often reminding their daughters that education was the key to their success in America and that they were grateful to have obtained one.

Cathy's parents also reminded their daughters that the buck did not stop with them—they wanted their daughters to excel even more. America was a land full of opportunities, and they had not traveled halfway across the world to have their children not take advantage of these opportunities. Cathy is now a surgeon in New York City. After Cathy's sister obtained her degree in engineering, Cathy's parents sold their home and moved into the home of their dreams, complete with swimming pool and tennis court. As we discussed in Secret 3, Cathy's parents were able to delay their own gratification (a lavish lifestyle) for the sake of their daughters' academic success.

Before you start feeling guilty about living in your beautiful home or driving a luxury car, rest assured that we believe there are many ways that you—like Cathy's parents—can raise self-motivated and academically gifted children. If you are fortunate enough to have lots of money, the key is to keep your money in perspective. Wealthy parents who show humility and an appreciation for their good fortune have a better chance at raising children who are self-motivated and successful in the classroom. Children of these parents will learn that financial security is earned through hard work, dedication, and character; they will see their parents donate time, energy, and money to charities and community outreach programs, and will likely derive the same happiness and fulfillment from doing so as their parents. They will learn that wealth alone does not guarantee professional and personal fulfillment. As a result, these children will work harder in the classroom. Remember, kids who lead a totally indulgent lifestyle at home will be less likely to work hard to overcome academic hurdles. Don't allow your child to believe that he or she is entitled to power, respect, and privilege by wealth alone. If nothing else, remember this: Don't foster this arrogance in your children.

Wealthy parents may find it difficult to teach their child to delay gratification if they live lavishly. Living more modestly (at least in front of their child) can improve parents' chances of raising a child who views higher education as the most effective means of securing financial and personal wealth.

We'd like to share with you another inspiring story of wealthy parents who managed to raise children who were self-motivated and successful in the classroom.

The "Ohs" were well-to-do Korean immigrants who had amassed a great deal of wealth by acquiring, one by one, a string of Dunkin' Donuts stores. Having lived in abject poverty for a good portion of their lives, they happily purchased a half-million dollar home on a sprawling golf course. Matching his-and-hers Mercedes soon followed. They went on dream vacations to Europe and the Caribbean, and enjoyed all that money could buy. They were living the American dream.

The Ohs had two sons whom we will call Albert and William. Although the two boys were surrounded by their parents' wealth, the Ohs made it very clear that the posh house and luxury cars were rewards *they* had earned for their sacrifice and hard work. Though they often expressed to their children that they were happy to provide them with advantages and opportunities other children did not have, by no means had the boys earned rights to their parents' fortune simply by being born into the family. Albert and William would have to work hard in order to one day be as financially secure as their parents.

Easier said than done! But the Ohs were adamantly opposed to spoiled, lazy children. They kept their children on a tight budget, dependent on completion of household chores and homework assignments. On one occasion, they left William, who had received a particularly poor report card, with his grandmother while the rest of the family went to Paris. The message was clear—the parents had earned the right to enjoy what their hard-earned money could buy, not the boys. With dedication and hard work, the boys could do the same for themselves in the future. Albert is currently a biomedical engineer in the Research Triangle; William is a high school chemistry teacher. Both love what they do and are grateful for the opportunities they were given.

Some of you readers may think what the Ohs did was harsh, but we disagree. Many children live in relative poverty, unable to travel within the United States, much less abroad. Wealthy parents who want to enjoy what their money can buy should not feel guilty about withholding rewards from their children when appropriate. If you are living in a mansion, your children are already experiencing something that most of their peers are not. Don't spoil their chances of experiencing the thrill of earning a nice living on their own. Success that is earned tastes much sweeter than success handed over on a silver platter.

We have shared with you stories of families from all socioeconomic backgrounds that have raised successful children in the classroom and in the workplace. As you can see, they all achieved academic and professional success. The key for parents is to teach children that they are entitled only to those things they work for, regardless of wealth.

Secret 12: To-Do List

- If you are part of a modest-income family, encourage your child to pursue careers that offer both personal fulfillment and financial reward. Teach him that happiness is in some part dependent on financial stability.
- If you are wealthy, provide your child with incentives to excel academically that are not financial in origin. These incentives may include (but are not limited to) increased self-esteem and family pride, a love of learning, a respect for higher education and the skills it imparts, and the satisfaction that comes from setting and achieving goals.
- Make your child pay for some, if not all, of his college education. This will instill in him an appreciation for how hard one has to work to make ends meet.
- Wealthy parents may find it difficult to teach their child to delay gratification if they live lavishly. Living more modestly (at least in front of their child) can improve their chances of raising a child who views higher education as the most effective means of securing financial and personal wealth.

Secret 13

Limit Extracurricular Activities That Interfere with Schoolwork

Children and teenagers are busier today than ever before. School-age children today juggle an astonishing number of extracurricular activities, ranging from sports to musical instruments to various after-school clubs. We recently met one high school junior who was involved in thirteen extracurricular activities! Just to name a few, she was on the varsity swimming and volleyball teams and was active in the yearbook, debate, young scientists, and math clubs. She also volunteered as a candy striper at a local hospital and nursing home once a week; in her spare time she headed up a teen Bible study group on Wednesday evenings. When we asked her why in the world she would spread herself so thin, her answer was frighteningly matter-of-fact: "I have to do all this. How else I am going to get into Harvard?"

Indeed, it appears tougher than ever to gain acceptance into a top university. Competitive colleges today no longer want the straight-A, 1600-on-the-SATs student with no extracurricular activities or personality; rather, they seem to want the straight-A, 1600-on-the-SATs student *with* a dozen extracurricular activities and a winning personality. And as the competition gets more fierce and students are enrolling in more extracurricular activities than they can handle, these colleges are seeing more of these academically gifted and well-rounded individuals.

So what's the problem, you might be asking? What's wrong with expecting your children to be more than just their 4.0 grade point averages and perfect SATs? Absolutely nothing, unless the laundry list of extracurricular activities starts detracting from their core education and running them ragged in the process.

That being said, we have yet to meet any student who is involved regularly in more than three extracurricular activities who heartily enjoys and excels in all of them. For example, it is not possible for Soo to be the best surgeon, writer, pianist, and tennis player she can be all at the same time. In order for Soo to concentrate on becoming a gifted surgeon, her medical training took precedence over her hobbies. While learning how to operate, Soo could no longer find an hour a day to write or thirty minutes a day to practice the piano. Her daily tennis excursion became a distant memory. Because Soo placed a higher level of importance on becoming a talented surgeon than on improving her piano, tennis, or writing skills, her surgical skills improved while her other skills languished. As much as she wished she could continue performing at a high level in all areas with minimal effort and time commitment, she could not. You can either choose to be extremely knowledgeable in a few areas or minimally knowledgeable in many, extremely talented in some venues or mediocre in all. It's your choice, but we opt for the former scenario.

Being the jack-of-all-trades generally equates to being the master of none.

Which is why we recommend having your children concentrate on their schoolwork and two to three extracurricular activities they enjoy, and scrap the rest. We believe in the well-rounded student as much as the college admissions staff does, but we don't believe it's necessary to participate in a million different activities to get into the college of one's choice. Furthermore, most colleges today would rather see a student who has a true passion and talent for one activity—even if it's an unusual one!—than a student who is only a half-hearted member of the "right" clubs. For example, a boy who creates and publishes his own comic book in school will be more appealing than a girl who is on the debate, math, and lacrosse teams, but who doesn't stand out in any of them.

As for what extracurricular activities to choose, it's most important for your child to be passionate about them. In general, however, we do recommend at least one sports activity, which offers health benefits, stress reduction, and a healthy sense of team spirit. If your child is at all musically inclined, we also strongly recommend a musical instrument, for reasons we will expand upon later. As for finding out what activities your child has a knack for and interest in, expose him early to a wide variety of activities. Our parents exposed us to golf, tennis, badminton, and swimming as a family early in childhood, and soon it became clear to them that our hearts and abilities lay in the tennis court, not on the driving range. If your child is participating in more than three extracurricular activities on a regular basis, chances are he's not excelling at any one. There's also a good chance his schoolwork is suffering on account of the time commitment required for these activities, which isn't going to help his chances of gaining admission to a competitive college. Lastly, when a child has too much on his plate and is being pushed in a million different directions, chances are he's not having fun or enjoying himself. And we all know what happens to the quality of work when a task becomes boring or is considered a chore.

To further impress upon you how destructive spreading oneself too thin with extracurriculars can be, we'd like to illustrate how busy the typical conscientious and college-aspiring student is already. We'll start with Soo's high school list of extracurricular activities, which included tennis, piano, and volunteering at a local hospital. Let's run through a typical day in Soo's high school life, which we believe is not dissimilar to the daily lives of many adolescent students. After school ended around three-thirty, Soo would have a few minutes to grab a snack and get changed for tennis practice. Tennis practice involved daily exercises from about four to five-thirty in the afternoon. That meant that by the time Soo got home, it was six in the evening. On days there was a tennis meet (competition with another school), Soo would often not get home until seven or seven-thirty. Dinner with the family would typically last until seven (eight on a meet day); by the time the dishes were cleaned, it would be seven-thirty. From seven-thirty to eight every evening, Soo would practice the piano, and once a week she would make a trip to her instructor's house for private lessons. So it would not be until eight or nine that Soo would finally get a chance to start her homework assignments, which were often quite plentiful. Homework was usually completed in an hour or hour and a half, after which Soo would spend the next half hour to an hour doing additional studies we discussed in depth earlier in the book. This would invariably take until nine-thirty or ten, after which our mother would come into the living room where Soo was trying to catch a few minutes of TV and tell her to go to bed.

Thinking back to those days, Soo wonders how she did it all. After all, she was only juggling three extracurricular activities in addition to her homework, and she still didn't have enough hours in the day to do all that she wanted, much less just to relax. Even the weekends were filled with extracurricular activities, from piano competitions to local tennis championships and volunteer work at a the hospital.

If Soo, who was juggling only three extracurricular activities during high school, could barely handle her load, we doubt that students handling more than two or three are not feeling completely overwhelmed. Let's face it—unless your teenager can work on minimal sleep (most can't, as we all know), there are just not enough hours in the day to adequately complete homework, participate in activities, and prepare for the next day. Notice that we use the word "adequately" in the last sentence, for good reason. Sure, it may be possible for a student to participate in three or four activities after school, get home late feeling exhausted and hungry, wolf down dinner, complete homework assignments, and wake up the next day to do it all over again. But that student won't be doing any of it well, or at least as well as he or she should be doing it. There is just not enough time in the day to complete each task to the best of one's ability.

Limit your child's extracurricular activities to two or three activities he or she shows both an interest in and a knack for.

Now you may be asking why one should take on any extracurricular activities at all. After all, wouldn't it be better for your children to come home directly from school and concentrate on their homework assignments and academic pursuits? Who needs sports or other interests, if they are going to get in the way of time spent studying?

Unfortunately, we know a few people who think this way (to tell you the truth, many are Asian!). These students are of the misguided belief that any activity not academically related is a waste of their time, and they will indeed rush home after school, skip dinner, and stay up late in order to study. But the truth is, all their efforts won't make them more attractive to college admissions personnel. Quite the contrary: most colleges prefer well-rounded, academically gifted students to the one-dimensional straight-A pupils. And by well-rounded we mean men and women who are personable, hold themselves to high moral and ethical standards, are team players, have many interests outside of academics, and are well liked and well regarded by their peers. A tall order, to say the least.

So why do top colleges favor these well-rounded individuals? Why is it that they would prefer a student with a 3.6 grade point average who coaches Little League on Saturdays and plays in a blues band in his free time to someone with a 4.0 grade point average with no interests outside the classroom? In the real world, a world that all students will someday join, the most "successful" people are not those who simply excel on the job. For example, the most successful physician is not necessarily the one who makes the most money, sees the most patients, or scored the highest on his medical boards. Most patients and even other physicians tend to consider physicians with thriving practices due to their affability and availability the most "successful." Rarely does a patient's opinion of his or her physician have anything to do with where the physician graduated from medical school and how well he scored on the MCATs (the standardized examination for medical school admission). On the other hand, the physician's bedside manner, compassion, and availability are important factors in determining the success of his or her practice.

An example that further illustrates this point involves a law school classmate of Jane's named Alice—a shy, sweet girl who often seemed scared of her own shadow. Unlike many other law students who were outspoken, Alice never volunteered in class. When she was called on, Alice would nervously whisper her answer while fiddling with her hair and turning a bright shade of red—she looked so uncomfortable that her peers often found it difficult even to watch her. It wasn't until the students selected for interviews with the top Philadelphia law firms were announced that everyone realized how high Alice's grades were. As one of the few students selected to interview (usually the top 10% to 15% of law school students), it seemed Alice was much more on top of her game than she appeared.

Yet despite receiving impressive grades and even making law review, Alice was the only top student who failed to receive a job offer after interviewing. Most students with grades as high as Alice's had their pick of law firms to work for. The truth is Alice didn't receive an offer because she was socially awkward and nervous, qualities her potential employers detected immediately. Despite her academic record, they simply could not envision clients trusting her or members of the firm working well with her. In the real world, one must play and interact well with others, and participating in extracurricular activities enables children to perfect this art.

It is important to remember that the key is to *limit* extracurricular activities, not exclude them from your child's life completely. While spreading your child too thin can be harmful, getting your child involved with a manageable extracurricular load will help him develop in ways you may not have expected. Recent studies have shown that involvement in extracurricular activities deters children from undesirable behavior (such as drugs, crime, etc.), boosts their self-image, develops social skills, fosters hidden talents, and prepares them for the hustle and bustle of daily life as adults.

So now that you know about the benefits, how should you introduce extracurricular activities to your child? Although letting your child pick the extracurricular activity of his or her choice may seem the obvious way to go, you would be surprised to know just how many parents force their children to pursue activities that suit their own interests rather than their child's. Just because you always wanted to take ballet lessons doesn't mean your daughter will gravitate toward leotards and tutus—pursuing activities that your child shows genuine interest in is crucial. After all, choosing what extracurricular activities to pursue may be one of the few decisions your child can actively participate in. As a parent, you are there to nurture, guide, and discipline your child, not control his or her destiny.

That being said, you should also be aware that some extracurricular activities have been shown to directly benefit other areas in your children's lives. Studies have indicated that students who participate in art activities are four times more likely to be recognized for academic achievement, four times more likely to participate in math and science fairs, three times more likely to hold student government positions, and three times more likely to win an award for school attendance. Participation in the arts also encourages creative thinking, language fluency, originality, and elaboration. In fact, students instructed in the arts have index scores averaging twenty points higher in these areas.

Try to incorporate at least one artistic extracurricular activity into your child's routine.

Looking back on our childhood, we vividly remember being dragged to piano and violin lessons at an early age. We were also heavily encouraged to express our creativity on paper, in the form of stories, plays, essays, and even books (our mom still has the copy of *Treasure Island* that Soo wrote and illustrated)! As we grew older, we realized that many of our Asian friends and colleagues had similar experiences. They, too, took piano, violin, ballet, and art lessons. These experiences have undoubtedly shaped the young adults we've become and have benefited us both academically and professionally. When we were younger, we assumed everyone played an instrument or took ballet lessons. Today, we realize that it's not simply a coincidence: most Asian parents provide their children with these types of lessons with a purpose. And that purpose has served us well.

In addition to preparing children for the real world, extracurricular activities can help keep your children out of trouble. In a day and age where peer pressure can be overwhelming, children with unsupervised time on their hands are more likely to fall prey to things like drugs, alcohol, and sex. Although our parents kept a watchful eye on us as we were growing up, it was impossible for them to know exactly what we were doing at every given moment. Between the two of us, our extracurricular activities included piano, violin, swimming, and tennis. While other children were dabbling in drinking and drugs, we were spending our time enjoying and perfecting our hobbies. For children growing up in poor urban areas, where poverty can breed violence and illicit drug and alcohol abuse, participation in extracurricular activities may be even more crucial. Today, many successful individuals involved in music, sports, and literature have overcome poverty and beat the odds as a result of their involvement in or passion for a particular extracurricular activity. Many have even admitted that while other children in the neighborhood were selling drugs or getting pregnant at an early age, their "craft" helped them rise above. Tennis phenoms Venus and Serena Williams are great examples of individuals who overcame poverty and achieved success due to guidance from their parents, as well as their own commitment to their sport.

Getting back to how participation in extracurricular activities prepares children for "the real world," one must be reminded that no one gets to the top alone. While getting straight A's and acing the SATs are largely individual efforts, throughout one's life the number of group successes will far exceed any individual ones. Behind every successful person are several individuals who helped him achieve success, and extracurricular activities like basketball, soccer, field hockey, theater, band, and the school newspaper are instrumental in teaching children the value of teamwork.

Through teamwork, children learn that the likelihood of success is greater when individuals work together toward a common goal. Relationships are nurtured and social skills are developed as children learn how to best interact with other members of the team. In that sense, extracurricular activities provided us with the foundation to work well with others, develop lasting relationships (both personal and at work), and value teamwork.

Children who participate in a couple of extracurricular activities (remember, not more than two or three!) will also learn firsthand how to multitask and manage their time efficiently. As fast-paced and hectic as today's world is, individuals who can acquire proficient multitasking and time-management skills have a greater chance of moving ahead in the world while keeping their sanity. These days, we often hear parents say they're exhausted from chauffeuring their children from one activity to another. Although it may be tiring (for both parents and their children), going from one activity to another does force one to prioritize and manage one's time wisely.

Juggling extracurricular activities will improve multitasking ability—an important skill to have in the real world.

In summary, extracurricular activities can enhance your child's interpersonal skills and increase his chances of being accepted into a top college. College admissions officers know what it takes to get ahead in the real world, and they want to fill their classrooms with men and women who will throw themselves into today's, dog-eat-dog world and come out on top.

Secret 13: To-Do List

- Being the jack-of-all-trades generally equates to being the master of none.
- Limit your child's extracurricular activities to two or three activities your child shows both an interest in and ability for.
- Try to incorporate at least one artistic extracurricular activity into your child's routine.
- Through teamwork, children learn that the likelihood of success is greater when individuals work together toward a common goal. Relationships are nurtured and social skills are developed through teamwork as children learn how to best interact with other members of the team. Extracurricular activities provided us with the foundation to work well with others, develop lasting relationships (both personal and at work), and value teamwork.
- Juggling extracurricular activities will improve multitasking ability—an important skill to have in the real world.

Secret 14

Promote an Environment of Healthy Competition

It is certainly no secret that an atmosphere of healthy competition brings out one's best effort and performance. Think the Olympic games, and how the performances of athletes are significantly advanced in such a setting. True, many athletes crumble under the intense pressure and scrutiny, but those who rise to the top often manage to surpass even their own expectations.

We recently enjoyed the movie *Seabiscuit* starring Jeff Bridges and Tobey Maguire, a movie that nicely illustrates the importance of competition in bringing out one's best performance. The star of the film is a hugely underrated racehorse named Seabiscuit who emerges the winner of prestigious local and national horse races. In one scene, Seabiscuit's jockey asks a fellow jockey to allow the racehorse to look his competitor in the eye shortly before the finish line. If Seabiscuit looks into the soul of his competitor, his jockey states, there's no way in hell he will lose the race. Indeed, after the jockey intentionally slows his horse down so that Seabiscuit can get a glimpse of his competition, Seabiscuit is able to muster a final and effective burst of energy to cross the finish line first. Even the fastest runner in the world will run faster if there is someone chasing him. Herein lies the importance of competition.

All parents have questions and concerns regarding the role and importance of competition in their children's lives, and rightly so. Too much competition can create anxiety and build resentment; not enough competition can prevent your children from going the extra mile. There is a fine line here, one that many well-meaning parents have unfortunately crossed.

Healthy competition can be beneficial for one's personal, emotional, and academic growth. All men and women can recall a situation in which competition brought out their best performances—think back to the time when you were struggling for that job promotion or running for class president. You worked harder and were more committed to achieving your goal because others were vying for the same position. When Jane was in grade school, her English teacher organized a writing competition. A prize would be given for the best short story. We recall her working really hard on that story to maximize her chance of winning. Sure, her English teacher could have assigned her students the task of writing a short story as homework. But she wanted to raise the bar and bring out her students' best performances by adding an element of competition, and she succeeded. Soon after the competition ended, Jane's teacher told us she was astounded by the quality of the work she had received. The mere addition of a prize had done wonders for the efforts put forth by the students. In fact, their creativity, grammar, and writing style had noticeably improved. Jane didn't end up winning, but we still remember how good her short story was.

How you define or view competition will ultimately determine your level of success in any endeavor. There are those who view competition as a frantic and harried race to the top; these individuals were taught that winning is all that matters. They seek only to win and will do whatever it takes to do so, regardless of who they step on along the way. Although these selfish bullies may be successful in their endeavors, they often find themselves alone at the top.

There are, on the other hand, individuals who accurately view competition as a healthy way to bring out one's best performance. These individuals enjoy being in the race and will put their best foot forward when competing for the prize. Although these individuals want to win (who doesn't?), their definition of winning is different from the selfish, destructive, and egomaniacal individuals we previously alluded to. Men and women who use competition wisely view winning as participating in a challenge and completing it to the best of their abilities, regardless of the outcome. They enjoy the thrill of competing as much as the next person, but mainly because their best performance emerges in this setting. They are not fixated on beating others or ultimately even on winning; rather, they are focused on setting a higher standard for themselves.

How your child views competition can significantly influence his academic performance as well as his emotional well-being. If you teach your child that winning is all that matters by shunning or criticizing him when he fails or doesn't meet your expectations, he will likely become unhappy and self-centered in addition to becoming a cutthroat competitor. Parents should reject this avenue and teach their child (preferably by example) that competition enhances performance and that those who enjoy the process and put forth their best efforts are the true winners. Our parents took this one step further. Not only did they want us to put our best foot forward, they also wanted us to strive to win. (In our experience, participating in sports really nutured our competitive spirits.)

Parents should use healthy competition to bring out their child's best effort *and* performance. A desire to win—within reason of course—is good for kids!

We can recall several stories that exemplify our parents' views on competition. One story in particular involves Soo and a high school mathematics competition. As you now know, our parents were intimately involved in every aspect of our education. As you are also now aware, we were far from rich while growing up. Although our parents encouraged Soo to strive for admission into the top universities, they were always worried about the costs. Many of the private universities Soo expressed interest in charged astronomical tuition rates, upwards of ten thousand dollars a semester. Our parents were in the unfortunate situation that many middle class Americans find themselves in—too rich for financial assistance but too poor to bear the cost comfortably.

Undeterred, our father began researching the financial aid and scholarship programs at the universities Soo was interested in attending early in her junior year. One of the schools was Duke University, a prestigious institution located only twenty minutes away from home (now you know why Soo didn't want to go there!). Nicknamed "the Harvard of the South," Duke was also one of the most expensive private universities. Tuition would be nearly ten thousand dollars a semester, and of course there would be additional room-and-board charges.

After some research, our father became aware of a scholarship program that would enable twenty North Carolina students to attend Duke University with their tuition fully paid. These students would be selected based on their performance in a statewide mathematics competition. Selected eleventh-grade students gifted in mathematics could compete for these scholarships, which would be awarded to the twenty highest scorers. However, the prize would not come easily: the test would feature math questions requiring mastery of college- and graduate-level concepts.

Our father always seized opportunities with gusto, and this situation was no different from any other. Soon enough, Soo was reviewing highly advanced mathematics concepts that were well beyond her years. Even our father, a math whiz himself, had considerable difficulty coming up with solutions to some of the sample questions. During the months leading up to the exam, Soo and our father purchased several books filled with sample items and previous test questions and answers and got down to business.

By the time Soo took the test, she had learned to grasp concepts she would revisit years later in advanced calculus classes at Johns Hopkins University. She gave it her all, but despite her best efforts, she didn't come close to winning that scholarship.

If our father was disappointed, he didn't show it. Although disappointed, Soo also handled the loss well. She might not have won the ultimate prize, but she had achieved something invaluable in the process. Years later she would have little difficulty grasping advanced Calculus III classes at Johns Hopkins while her peers toiled for hours only to receive marginal grades. In the end, Soo received an A with minimal effort (which left her more time to have fun and attend parties), largely due to her and our father's efforts years ago.

Have your child adopt the attitude that losing in one competition can help him win in another—if he learns from his mistakes.

Life is a series of competitions. Right from the beginning, children are encouraged to beat out other children at school and in sports. The winners advance to prestigious private schools and Ivy League–caliber universities. In college, the competition becomes even more fierce. Only those with top grades and stellar test scores are able to enter certain professions. Rest assured, competition hardly ends in the workplace; adult professionals seem to endlessly compete for that next promotion or raise. Academics aside, there is competition to woo the best-looking and most intelligent mate. There is competition to own the nicest car, the biggest house. Women compete to own the best wardrobe, have the slimmest figure, and marry the most doting husbands. After marriage, children bring out parents' competitive spirits once again; now the weary parents get to watch the cycle repeat itself.

Which brings us to our next important topic—how to get your child comfortable with competing. You will be doing your child a disservice by not teaching him the art of competing successfully, and in a way that is healthy for his morale. Again, we mentioned earlier how to teach your child to view competition; now we'd like to discuss some strategies as to how to get your child to maneuver comfortably in the rat race.

Once you are comfortable that your child views winning as putting forth his best effort and learning something valuable in the process, you can begin to involve your child in competitive activities. A great place to start is with activities outside the classroom. For us, these centered around sports and the arts (musical instruments). As we discussed in the previous chapter, extracurricular activities are a great way to foster a spirit of teamwork—but they're also a great way to encourage a little healthy competition!

Our parents wanted their daughters to be comfortable in their roles as competitors. They were committed to raising daughters who loved to compete because of the personal growth that occurred in the process—regardless of the outcome. As we have mentioned, we have many fond childhood memories of playing tennis and the piano (Soo played the violin for a short time, but even my parents couldn't tolerate the awful noises she created). When Soo turned five, our parents invested in a used piano to showcase in our living room. They found a nice piano teacher in our apartment building, and Soo started weekly half-hour lessons. Our piano teacher suggested practicing for a half hour each day, so at an early age Soo learned discipline. Imagine how hard it is to sit still for thirty minutes at a piano when you are only five! But that's beside the point—this chapter is about competition, not discipline.

Our involvement in piano and tennis offered us numerous opportunities to compete with our peers. Several times a year our piano teacher held recitals, where each child would have the chance to showcase his or her talent. When we were older, we even had the opportunity to compete in local and statewide piano competitions. As frivolous as we may view these little competitions now, at the time, they loomed large in our young minds. Jane recalls her heart beating fast and her hands getting clammy prior to playing the piano in front of judges; Soo recalls the adrenaline rush while preparing for a tennis match against a particularly strong opponent. We recall dreading these events early on, when our nerves would get the best of us. We even wanted to bow out on occasion, but our parents never let our fears predominate. They would urge us back into the ring gently, reminding us that our temporary suffering was well worth the heightened self-confidence and competitive spirit we would be rewarded with in the end. We were always taught to envision future successes and accomplishments; it was often just this small taste of success that would push us across the finish line.

Our parents also knew that practice makes perfect. The more we played the piano, the better we would become. In the same vein, they knew the more competitions we participated in, the more comfortable we would be with the art of competing. And they were right—with every competition our anxiety lessened and our confidence soared. Whether or not we ultimately won, we were always treated as winners. Because of our parents' positive mentality, the fear of humiliation and failure never did grip us.

Life is a series of competitions, so the best way to get your kids comfortable competing is to immerse them in activities that develop their competitive spirits. Remember, practice makes perfect!

Which leads us to the most powerful destroyer of healthy competition and ultimately, of success: the fear of humiliation. Many psychologists claim that the fear of humiliation is one of the most powerful destroyers of the human spirit. Along these lines, recent polls have revealed that public speaking—fear of humiliation in front of others—is the leading fear among Americans, even surpassing that of illness or death.

Although we were initially surprised by the results of this poll, it now makes sense to us: illness and/or death are inevitable; on the other hand, humiliation is often self-inflicted and can be avoided. For example, if you never try to get that promotion, you'll never get turned down for it. If you never ask him on a date, you'll never get rejected. If you never apply to that top university, you'll never receive a rejection letter. Imagine how little mankind would accomplish if we all led our lives like that—dreams would forever remain just a figment of our imaginations.

One of the best things our parents did was teach us to overcome our fears of failure, rejection, and humiliation. As they encouraged us to pursue our dreams, the possibility of failure was never mentioned; why would it be, when failure is never a result of any significant and full-hearted effort? Throughout all of our childhood "competitions," our parents always concentrated on what we had learned *this time* and what we might do differently the *next time.*

That way, the outcomes of our competitions were always successes; they never gave the crippling fears of failure, rejection, and humiliation a chance to develop in us.

Of course, being a good competitor doesn't mean you'll never feel afraid. We often felt afraid growing up, but the important thing was, our parents taught us never to let fear stop us from accomplishing our goals. We remember our mother telling us that fear is a great motivator as long as it doesn't paralyze you. Perhaps we all can recall a time in our lives when we were able to channel our nervous energy and pull off the performance of our lives. Your children are more likely to become successful competitors if you acknowledge that a certain amount of fear is normal.

Fear is a great motivator, as long as you don't let it paralyze you.

Years later, we are strong competitors. Jane's hands no longer get clammy before a big meeting; Soo's heart rate barely quickens before giving a talk to a large audience. Early on, we learned to handle stage fright through numerous piano recitals; we learned how to get our competitive juices flowing long ago by competing in tennis meets. Most important, we learned to lose gracefully and to always view ourselves as winners. Today we are young women who never shy away from tackling a difficult situation or attempting to defy the odds. Thanks to our parents, we possess the self-confidence to know we can beat them.

Secret 14: To-Do List

- Parents should use competition to bring out their child's best effort *and* performance. A desire to win is healthy!
- Have your child adopt the attitude that losing in one competition can only help him win in another—if he learns from his mistakes.
- Life is a series of competitions, so the best way to get your kids comfortable competing is to immerse them in activities that will develop their competitive spirits. Remember, practice makes perfect.
- Fear is a great motivator, as long as you don't let it paralyze you.

Secret 15

Surround Your Children with Similarly Minded Friends and Role Models

This is one of the most difficult tasks a parent faces. How are you supposed to keep track of the kids your child is hanging out with at school? Especially in this day and age of increased defiance and independence in our children—and increasingly hectic adult schedules—this task seems formidable indeed. Granted, it has never been easy for parents to tell their children who to hang out with (or date, for that matter). As we know, parents who insist that their children halt relations with peers they consider to be bad influences are often met with heavy resistance.

But the fact remains, who your children choose to hang out with is crucial to their academic success. This is particularly true when your children are teenagers. The older your children get, the less they want to listen to you—they're more likely to see you as barriers to independence than fountains of wisdom. Because teens turn to friends, not you, for guidance, as parents you want to make sure the kids providing that guidance share your child's values and goals.

Soo's friends throughout grade school, high school, and college were all very similar in personality and goals. Most were quiet by nature and considered good listeners; all were driven to excel in the classroom, were confident in their abilities, and were never ones to shy away from challenges. They never got into any trouble with the law, and most had good relationships with their parents.

Jane had a more diverse group of friends. She mingled with more free spirits—teenagers who occasionally smoked cigarettes, drank, and partied on weekends. In spite of that fact, Jane stayed far away from those who openly defied their parents or other authorities . . . and far away from those who believed education was a waste of their precious time. Among her close high school friends, all went on to four-year universities, and about half went on to graduate school.

So how did we know to avoid the troublemakers, the children who would lead us astray? By the time we hit our teens the personality traits that we admired and lived by were deeply ingrained in us, so we gravitated toward those with similar ethics. Our parents started shaping us early, instilling in us the values we needed to look for in our friends. They did not simply sit us down and tell us whom we could and could not hang out with, nor did they constantly harass us to befriend students based on intelligence, family values, and strong moral character. They knew that strategy would have backfired. Also, they never discouraged us from forming culturally or socioeconomically diverse circles of friends. On the contrary, they encouraged us to learn from other cultures and socioeconomic backgrounds. However, they were firm in their belief that we should befriend those with strong moral character and principles, who like us had a strong desire to excel in the classroom.

Subtly, almost without our knowledge, our parents gently yet firmly encouraged us to surround ourselves with girls and boys that acted and thought like us. When we were enrolled in preschool, our parents threw us birthday parties, to which they invited the entire class. At these parties, twelve to fifteen toddlers and their parents would show up and mingle with our parents over cake and ice cream. After spending several hours with them at our house (or at Chuck E. Cheese's or Pizza Hut), our parents would get a good idea which parents (and therefore which children) they believed would serve as good role models for their two impressionable daughters. Later on, these parents and their children would be the ones our parents would try to get to know better.

After the initial "screening" birthday party, the selected individuals would be invited out to dinner, or over to our modest home. Over good food and wine, the adults would share stories about work or parenthood, while their children played together. We befriended several bright and amiable boys and girls in this fashion, and our parents developed lasting friendships as well. If you're not into birthday parties, rest assured there are countless ways of identifying parents and kids with values similar to your own. For example, why not send out invitations to an outing at a museum, library, or a concert? Parents who place a high value on learning and education are more likely to take you up on your offer than parents who don't.

Parents are indicators of priorities in kids. Get to know them!

Essentially, our early birthday parties served as a means of screening out children and parents who did not have the same interests as our family. This is not to say that our parents thought they were better than others or that they believed their methods of childrearing were superior. They simply wanted to maintain control. It's hard enough to instill strong principles and a healthy work ethic at home, so why take the chance that your kids pick up bad habits at school? Or worse, from other parents? Our friends' parents wanted to raise children who were honest, kind, and emotionally well adjusted; they also made sure their children viewed academic excellence as a top priority. After all, we were spending more time with these children than with anyone else outside of the classroom. There *is* strength in numbers, no matter how strong an individual is or how valid a principle appears.

Make it your business to find out as much as you can about your young child's friends and their families. After getting to know the parents, encourage your child to spend more time with peers whose parents value education.

As we grew older, we naturally gravitated to other students who thought and acted like us: the students who took their grades seriously, who prepared in advance for tests, and who weren't afraid to excel in the classroom. These students were proud of their goals and realized that academic excellence would take them much further than fleeting popularity.

So, what happens if you haven't done the greatest job of screening out your children's friends? Is it too late? Well, it's better late than never. Parents need to be reminded that they have every right to tell their children what to do and whom to hang out with. This may sound harsh, but parents today are way too lenient when they set ground rules, often fearing their children will resent them or rebel even more. When it comes to young minds, the earlier children learn concepts, the better. Teach your children the value of surrounding themselves with positive role models and well-behaved, ambitious peers early. Never be afraid to tell them to stop spending so much time with "boys who do drugs" or girls more interested in their hair and make-up than their grades. Don't be discouraged if your children don't listen to you right off the bat, or if they meet your requests with considerable resistance. It will take time for them to see the reasoning behind your demands. Whatever they do or say, however, you have to stick to your guns.

Remember that you have every right to tell your children what to do and whom to hang out with—within reason, of course.

Energy and enthusiasm are hugely contagious. The more your children surround themselves with others who set lofty goals and have the energy to pursue them, the more likely they will be to follow suit. After all, nobody likes to be the odd man out. Surrounding ourselves with bright and motivated peers often inspired us to set the bar high rather than shoot for mediocrity.

The opposite is also true. If your children have friends who are slackers or terrible students, they may slack off in their own studies. Even if you instill the desire to succeed in your kids, if your children compare their grades or behavior to that of their underachieving friends, they may fool themselves into believing they're excelling when they're not. Our parents always told us that it's better to finish last in a race of winners than first in a race of losers. Looking back, we think those are very wise words indeed.

When your children are surrounded by peers who are positive role models, they'll be more likely to excel. Although there were a handful of individuals who inspired Jane to follow her dreams, her older sister Soo was most instrumental in helping her achieve her ultimate goal. For as long as Jane could remember, she wanted to be an author. Despite discouragement from many who firmly believed there were already too many starving writers in New York City, Jane wrote numerous articles, short stories, and essays in the hopes of getting published or winning a contest. Every now and then she would get positive feedback (she won one thousand dollars in an essay contest!), but most of the responses were standard form letters telling her to try again. After what seemed like a hundred rejection letters later, Jane slowly found herself becoming disheartened. Perhaps what others were telling her was true—maybe she would never become a published author.

In addition to wanting to become a physician, Soo also had dreams of becoming a writer while growing up. She had always enjoyed mystery novels, devouring Patricia Cornwell and Robin Cook novels almost as soon as they appeared in bookstores. During her final year as a surgical resident, Soo decided to write a medical thriller entitled *Heart Block* during her free time. Two months later, her first novel was completed. Not too shabby for a chief resident and first-time author, don't you think?

After the novel was completed, Soo began sending out query letters to various literary agents and publishers. She was deluged with rejection letters, and often joked that she had enough letters to wallpaper her entire bedroom. Eventually, a small publisher offered to publish *Heart Block*. Although Soo made absolutely no money from sales, she was now a published author. More importantly, Soo's small accomplishment became the motivation for both her and Jane to strive to become published authors with a reputable New York publisher.

Like-minded peers and role models provide the encouragement one needs to make it to the finish line. Growing up, Soo was always aware of Jane's dreams of becoming a writer. "You're the one who writes well," Soo would always insist. "If I had talent like you, I'd have written two novels by now. Don't waste your gifts." Despite Jane's annoyance at what she thought was constant badgering by a know-it-all older sister, Soo's words eventually did strike a chord. Motivated by the completion of Soo's first novel and her constant encouragement, Jane finally finished a children's book and began writing a humorous novel about a young woman in her twenties trying to adjust to "real life" after graduate school. Although her books were never published (not yet, anyway!), Jane was inspired by watching Soo complete and publish her own novel. Often, watching someone close to you reach for the stars and succeed pushes you to reach for the stars yourself. Years after *Heart Block* was completed, Soo and Jane worked together to complete *Top of the Class*. This time around, we managed to fulfill our dreams.

Learning to recognize when a friendship is no longer mutually beneficial or a when friend is no longer a role model or exemplary peer is also important. Every now and then, friendships that were once fulfilling can become detrimental. As parents of young children, you are responsible for spotting these deteriorating friendships and cutting them off. You need to lay the groundwork so that as your kids become young adults, they are able to recognize when time, distance, and differing perspectives on life in general turn a solid friendship into a shaky one. Our parents were always quick to encourage separation from individuals who might influence us negatively; in fact, they continued to express their opinions regarding our friendships even while we were in our twenties.

Even the oldest and strongest of friendships can change over time. If your child's friend is no longer a positive influence, the friendship should end.

Jane experienced this firsthand with a close friend from college named Darcie. When Jane was a freshman, the two young women met and instantly clicked. Soon they were staying up late night after night watching movies, discussing their dreams and plans for the future, and talking about boys. For two years they were practically inseparable. When Jane transferred to University of North Carolina at Chapel Hill her junior year, both girls were devastated and vowed to keep in touch. In the beginning, they remained true to their word, talking on the phone religiously and managing to spend birthdays and spring breaks together. When Jane entered law school, however, things changed dramatically.

In her first year of law school, Jane suddenly found herself with very little free time. After a rigorous day of classes, Jane could no longer spend her afternoons and evenings relaxing—her free time was now spent hitting the books or preparing for exams. Many nights she would even fall asleep with a book on her chest and highlighter in hand, the work seemingly only half finished. Darcie, on the other hand, began bartending at a local restaurant and bar after graduating college. Because Darcie worked in the evenings and on weekends, the two friends found it difficult to keep in touch regularly. Because of the difference in schedules, Jane recalls a few occasions when Darcie would call her at twelve-thirty or one in the morning, wanting to catch up.

The first few times Darcie called, Jane didn't mind the late hour—she was eager to know what was going on in her friend's life and missed the fun they used to have together. However, a few several-hour-long conversations later, it became clear that all Darcie wanted to talk about was her boyfriend. Jane was also finding it more difficult to concentrate during class after these self-imposed "all-nighters," a fact she relayed to our parents.

While our parents certainly expressed their concern over Jane's now-strained relationship with Darcie, in the end, Jane made the decision to stop her friend from affecting her schoolwork. One evening when Darcie called, Jane told her friend she wouldn't be able to talk past midnight on weekdays, as it was negatively affecting her law school studies. Suffice it to say that Darcie was completely taken aback—during college she and Jane had stayed up many nights until three or four in the morning, and the late night conversations had never affected Jane's studies. Why would it now? While Darcie felt that Jane was no longer interested in being a supportive friend, Jane felt that Darcie was being inconsiderate and disrespectful of her new role as a struggling law student. In retrospect, the main reason this friendship did not last was because the two women no longer had similar goals; while Darcie still wanted to have fun and could allow her relationship issues to far outweigh her professional goals in importance, Jane had committed to a grueling three years of law school in order to get her professional life in order. The moral of the story is, the more similar your goals are to those of your closest friends and family, the more likely you are to achieve them. There is no other way to put it.

Another close friend of Jane's from high school remains one of her best friends a decade later. As we mentioned earlier, Jane lived with her best friend Shannon and her family in Tokyo during a part of her senior year. After graduating from high school, the two girls attended colleges in different states. When Jane was in law school, Shannon attended business school. Although far apart, the girls kept in touch and managed to see each other once a year. Because Shannon and Jane had similar goals and aspirations, they always understood each other's time commitments and restraints. When Jane was feeling upset about a mediocre grade or a not-so-stellar presentation, Shannon understood and could sympathize. When Shannon had to cancel a visit at the last minute because she did not feel adequately prepared for an examination, Jane also understood. After completing her Master of Business Administration, Shannon enrolled in law school where she is completing her first year, and Jane now gives her friend valuable advice on how to survive the grueling first year. Today, both women remain extremely close, in large part due to the fact that they share similar views on the importance of education and career. In addition, our parents always strongly approved of Jane's friendship with Shannon.

Looking back, this stamp of approval only strengthened the friendship between the two. Believe it or not, kids do listen to some of what their parents say!

It goes without saying that close friends are an invaluable resource—not only do they make us laugh and give us the necessary emotional support during rough times, but they also provide us with the ability to look at things from a different perspective. We'd like to take a minute to thank our friends for always offering words of encouragement and giving us that extra push when we needed it most. And we'd like to thank our parents for guiding us to those friends in the first place!

Looking back, our friends had a great impact on our academic performance and success. After all, we learned from them, confided in them, and studied with them. Their goals became ours, and vice versa. We cheered each other on in times of success and encouraged each other in times of failure. Most important, we set the bar high, challenging each other to set new standards of excellence and accept no less than the best we could achieve. As parents, don't forget how important it is to foster those kinds of relationships. They truly make a world of difference.

Secret 15: To-Do List

- Make it your business to find out as much as you can about your young child's friends and their families. After getting to know the parents, encourage your child to spend more time with peers whose parents value education.
- Remember that you have every right to tell your children what to do and whom to hang out with—within reason, of course.
- Even the oldest and strongest of friendship can change over time. If your child's friend is no longer a positive influence, the friendship should end.

Secret 16

Help Your Child View America as a Great Land of Opportunity

Like the majority of Americans, we are thrilled to be living in this great country where the standard of living is unparalleled and the opportunities boundless. To give credit where credit is due, however, it was our parents who instilled in us this wondrous respect for our country. Their excitement and gratefulness to be here translated into our enthusiasm to seize opportunities that very few people on the planet are afforded.

If we had a dime for every time we heard our parents say, "We came here so we could give you a better life," we would be millionaires. As we mentioned previously, our parents came from humble beginnings. Our father was a high school math teacher in rural Korea with dreams of getting a graduate degree in the United States, our mother an aspiring college student. Because Korea at the time was (and to some extent still is) plagued by economic uncertainty and poor wages, our father jumped at the chance to obtain his master's degree in computer science at the University of Southern California. Weeks after obtaining his acceptance letter, our parents gathered up their few possessions, left all family and friends, and flew to America with only two hundred dollars in their pockets.

Our parents may have had big dreams, but their early life in America was far from glamorous. They rented a small one-bedroom apartment right on campus and both took low-paying jobs to make ends meet. Our father attended classes during the day and worked as a gas station attendant and janitor at night. Our mother worked twelve- to fourteen-hour days as a seamstress in a stifling factory with a dozen other immigrant women. She worked up until the day before she gave birth to Soo, never complaining about the hazardous working conditions or meager pay. To this day, it amazes us that our parents were able to stay focused on the future despite language barriers, cultural discrimination, and poverty.

In our humble opinion, children in America do not realize how good they have it. We recently caught an Oprah show that described the mistreatment of women around the world, watching in horror as Indian women were burned alive by their husbands when they were unable to provide "adequate" dowries. After watching this clip and others like it, we recall Oprah saying to the audience that "a woman born in America is truly the luckiest woman in the world." Well, along those same lines, we believe that any child born in America is the luckiest child in the world.

For many, an American childhood is still far from perfect; however, American children are born to a higher standard of living than the vast majority of children throughout the world. While children around the world are worrying about where to find their next meal, American children are eating all day long. In his Emmy-award winning *Bring the Pain*, comedian Chris Rock jokes that Americans have such an overabundance of food that they develop allergies to Food. "You'll never see a lactose-intolerant kid in Rwanda!" he barks. While children around the world are dying from diseases that are easily preventable through immunizations and access to routine health care, American children are playing Little League and soccer. While children around the world are being sold into slavery, prostitution, or arranged marriages before they hit puberty, American children are receiving an education in the safety of their classrooms. Now, we know those examples are harsh. It's not that we want to make American kids feel guilty just for being born in this country. We just want them to have an understanding of how different life could be.

As children growing up in America, we never thought twice about how lucky we were. Like other children, we complained when our parents told us we couldn't have a television in our rooms or when they enforced what we thought was an overly strict curfew. When our mother put dinner on the table and it wasn't to our liking, we rarely (if ever) thought about children in other parts of the world who were starving. We had known no other way of living and had little reason to believe that our lives were significantly better than 99% of the world. Thankfully, a few trips outside of the United States changed all of this.

If you ask Soo, she will tell you that her view of the world changed dramatically when she was twelve. It was the summer after her seventh grade, and our mother was going to visit her family in South Korea, who she hadn't seen in over a decade. Our mother originally planned on going by herself, but after thinking it over, our parents decided that Soo should accompany her. After considerable kicking and screaming (what twelve-year-old wants to leave friends and the comforts of home behind for a foreign country?), Soo boarded the plane and took the sixteen-hour flight to Seoul.

And what a month it turned out to be. Although Seoul is currently an internationally renowned city replete with culture and amenities, it was considerably less modern twenty years ago. Cities outside of Seoul, the nation's capital, were particularly slow to modernize. Our mother's older sister lived on the outskirts of Seoul in a modest three-bedroom home for its six members (the parents plus four daughters). To Soo's dismay, the home had only one bathroom (unheard of with five women in the house!). To make matters worse, a hole in the ground in an outhouse several yards from the house served as the only "toilet." Although there was a bathtub, there was no running hot water. Cold water was boiled and then cooled to the appropriate temperature every time someone needed to bathe.

Soo spent the first few days overseas extremely homesick and angry with our mother for insisting she visit Korea. After all, Soo was used to her own room, running hot water, and a comfortable bed. In Korea, Soo slept next to our mother on sleeping bags in the living room of our aunt's house. The girl who loved to take long, hot, thirty-minute showers (she still does), had to make do with one-minute "showers" that consisted of our mother manually rinsing the shampoo from her hair with warm water recently boiled in a pot. As for the outhouse—well, Soo still won't talk much about that experience.

Prior to traveling to Korea, Soo never got the chance to realize that her very middle-class, no-frills life in North Carolina was filled with modern conveniences and luxuries that the majority of the world would never experience. Things Soo took for granted were out of reach for most Koreans living outside of Seoul, yet they seemed happy with the quality of their lives.

The experience changed Soo forever. What she learned (and knows to this day) is that Americans are among the luckiest people in the world. Soo now feels grateful for rights she used to take for granted, such as access to health care and freedom of choice and speech.

After Soo returned from Korea, her newfound awareness of just how privileged she was fueled her desire to succeed and completely rejuvenated her already strong work ethic. Soo came to understand that teenagers around the world just like her had to worry about a lot more than she did. While she worried about getting good grades, playing the piano and tennis, and performing a few household chores, other teenagers were worrying about supporting their families and staying healthy. She now fully grasped the privilege of a first-rate education and the endless opportunities it afforded, on both a personal and financial level. Soo was one of the lucky few in the world, and she wasn't about to blow her chance to make a difference in the world.

Living overseas made Jane realize how fortunate she was to be a woman in America. As you know, Jane attended an international high school in Tokyo, Japan. Although Tokyo is similar to America in terms of economic wealth, Jane was surprised to learn that the "glass ceiling" is even lower for women in Japan. Unlike America, Japan is still very much a male-dominated society, where women are not given the same career choices and advancement opportunities as their male counterparts. Although Japan has an equal opportunity law, female graduates from top universities often find themselves being pushed into secretarial-type positions or jobs with little or no advancement opportunities. Most Japanese employers expect women to quit their jobs once they marry or have children, and therefore view hiring women in management-level positions as short term and risky. On the other hand, women who do pursue careers and forego or delay marriage and children are often viewed as radical feminists and are shunned by Japanese society.

After living in Japan, Jane realized that being a woman in America with all its perks and opportunities is a privilege too many of us take for granted. This is not to say that American women do not face many challenges in their family lives and in the workplace—they do. Despite the difficulties women in America still face climbing the corporate ladder, however, America has made great strides in gender equality and women's rights, and is currently decades ahead of most countries. Women in America can vote, file for divorce, and purchase and use contraception; in America women can be doctors, judges, police officers, newscasters, or astronauts. Realizing that there were a plethora of opportunities for women in America opened Jane's eyes to all that she could accomplish. Today when Jane feels like complaining about her job, she reminds herself just how fortunate she is to have a law degree and working in a field she is passionate about.

You've now read how visiting (for Soo) and living (for Jane) in another country changed our perspectives on the types of opportunities we had growing up in America. If you have the ability to do so, we strongly recommend sending your children overseas to experience different cultures and ways of life.

A child born in America is among the luckiest children in the world. The best way to get your child to realize this fact is to send him or her overseas to experience different cultures and ways of life, if you can afford it.

That being said, we realize many families are not in the position to spend hundreds (or thousands) or dollars on an international visit. If you find yourself in this predicament, there are still other ways to instill in your children an appreciation for all the opportunities that America affords most of its citizens.

For starters, you can inspire your children to volunteer their time helping the less fortunate. Our parents always stressed the importance of volunteering when we were young, and we often found ourselves reluctantly dragged to various soup kitchens and nursing homes alongside our parents. Food drives, homeless shelters, foster homes, and big brother/big sister mentorship programs are only a few of the many volunteer opportunities that are available in most cities. Although America is one of the wealthiest countries in the world, we know all too well that there are many areas that are downright impoverished. Yes, that's right—there are even places in America that do not have running water and flushing toilets, and there are areas that could be considered "war zones"—areas that are riddled with gunfire in the middle of the afternoon. The individuals living in these areas face additional challenges and hurdles that many of us only read about or watch on television. By volunteering, your children can learn firsthand how lucky they are and how many opportunities they have . . . all without leaving the country.

Other ways to get your kids to appreciate the opportunities given to them and to motivate them to take advantage of those opportunities is to encourage volunteering in the community to help the less fortunate, or to host foreign exchange students.

If volunteering isn't your or your child's cup of tea and you can't afford to travel out of the country, consider inviting an exchange student to live with you for a while. When Jane was in middle school, her friend Natalie hosted a Russian exchange student one summer. The purpose of the exchange was for the student to learn English and get a feel for life in America, while the host family in turn learned about Russian life and culture. Within days of the Russian student's arrival, Natalie found herself surprised by the mundane things her new friend considered luxurious and astounding. Natalie's house was a modest home equipped with two full bathrooms and three television sets; after meals were completed, leftovers were routinely given to the family dog. In Russia, the exchange student explained, these things were unheard of—most houses had only one bathroom and sometimes there wasn't enough food to go around for dinner for the family alone, much less the family pet! Halfway through the summer, Natalie's appreciation for her life in America was in full force. Jane recalls overhearing Natalie reprimanding their friends when they threw away portions of their lunches or complained about not receiving enough allowance. Hosting an exchange student is another great way to increase your children's awareness of other cultures without ever leaving the country.

Aside from volunteering and hosting an exchange student, another method to get your children to appreciate the wealth of opportunities they have in America is to simply sit them down and tell them how blessed they are. Share your own personal stories of tough periods in your life (that they did not have to experience) and how you persevered. Parents today often don't do this enough and may be surprised to find how willing their children are to listen.

One afternoon while we were in middle school, our parents sat us down and told us of their struggle to make ends meet in Korea and how they made new lives for themselves in America. We remember having mixed feelings at the time—we were sad for our parents for having been separated from their family and friends, yet we admired them for taking a risk and making something out of nothing. Most of all, however, we were appreciative of all the sacrifices they had made for us. Compared to our parents, we had it so easy! That day, the two of us made a vow to try our best to take advantage of all the opportunities afforded us and not complain so much. Many years later, we believe we have stayed true to our vow.

Many of our Asian-American friends, as well as some of the high-profile Asian-Americans mentioned in this book, credit their successes to their parents' perseverance and sacrifice. After all, if their parents succeeded despite the overwhelming odds; why shouldn't they? This mentality is engrained in Asian-Americans from a very early age and plays a large role in our success.

Sophia Choi, a prominent anchor for CNN Headline News, shares the sentiments of many Asian-Americans. She writes, "I credit my mother for giving me the strength of mind to handle the quick-paced nature of broadcasting and life in general. My mother never sat still. She was either asleep or going full speed. At times, she seemed a blur as she sped from home to shop then to the bank and back to the shop. Busy, busy, busy. Her motivation for all that running around: raising her three girls. As a widower, she had to make enough money. As a foreigner, she knew it would take twice the energy. As the sole owner of a wig shop, she knew it meant working day and night. The lesson she gave me did not come in the form of some big talk. It came from watching her all those years. She set an example for me and perfectly illustrated this lesson: do whatever it takes to beat, not meet, expectations. Thanks to her, I am a productive adult who stays busy, busy, busy." In other words, she believed that if her mother was able to make ends meet despite humble beginnings, she had better take advantage of the opportunities provided to her and excel.

Of course, you don't have to be an immigrant to share stories similar to the ones we just mentioned. Every parent has stories of perseverance and overcoming the odds, and these stories should be passed down to your children. All children can benefit from hearing how their parent or parents handled tough periods in their lives and ultimately triumphed, despite obstacles. By learning how you successfully handled hardship, your child might not view obstacles as quite so formidable.

Raise your children with the view that America is a land of opportunity. Encourage and try to provide opportunities for your children to experience other cultures. This is the best way to get them to fully grasp the wealth of opportunities that are available to them. In a land as full of opportunities as America, your kids would be foolish not to take advantage of them; stressing this fact is not only wise, but also crucial to their future successes.

Secret 16: To-Do List

- A child born in America is among the luckiest children in the world. The best way to get your child to realize this fact is to send him overseas to experience different cultures and ways of life (if you can afford it).
- Other ways to get your kids to appreciate the opportunities given to them and to motivate them to take advantage of those opportunities is to encourage volunteering in the community to help the less fortunate, or to host a foreign exchange student.

Secret 17

Accept Responsibility with Your Children for Their Failures at School

Every day on television, we watch shows focusing on the lives of courageous men and women who overcame poverty, broken homes, and lack of support from family and friends to make it big. America is a country that believes in the individual. After all, everyone roots for the underdog, and we are no different.

You just have to glance at a TV programming schedule to see how individualism is given priority over the team in American popular culture. Just take a look at today's leading TV shows such as *The Apprentice* and *Survivor*. Both start with two teams competing against one another for the ultimate prize—either a high-paying job working for Donald Trump or a million dollars. Although the majority of each episode is devoted to watching teams work together toward a common goal, the last (and undoubtedly most exciting) minutes are spent watching the members of the losing team "rat out" their teammates for survival. Although the last individual standing has won the prize in part because of his teammates, the team effort is rarely acknowledged. In a culture that places little trust or value on the team or group, often viewing it merely as a stepping stone to individual success, it comes as no surprise that we celebrate individual triumphs above group ones. In America, there is room for only one winner, and winner takes all.

It makes sense that with this belief in the power of the individual comes a lack of shared responsibility. When an individual succeeds, he or she is given full credit for the achievement; on the other hand, when an individual fails, he or she is expected to take full responsibility for the wrongdoing. Fair? Perhaps, but we all know that one does not succeed or fail entirely on one's own.

When children are young, parents often take responsibility for their achievements as well as their failures. When a toddler misbehaves at a restaurant, diners shoot disapproving looks to the parents, not the toddler. As evidenced by their sheepish grins and apologetic smiles, the parents understand that their toddler's behavior (or misbehavior) is their responsibility. On a similar note, children's successes such as mastery of the alphabet or learning to ride a bike are shared between children and parents. No child learns to ride a bike or recite the alphabet alone, and parents understand the importance of their role in the achievement of these milestones.

As children grow, however, the parent-child relationship changes dramatically. Children are no longer viewed as direct extensions of their parents, and vice versa. Parents are encouraged to foster individual accountability in their kids so that they learn to take responsibility for their own actions and become independent. Independence, after all, is what Americans crave above almost all things. Just go to the nearest McDonald's and you'll see a dozen kids age fifteen and sixteen working for minimum wage to buy a car or save for college. Many American children leave home well before their eighteenth birthdays (often with their parents' blessing), craving their independence long before they are able to emotionally and financially support themselves. And while it is noble for a child to attempt to take full responsibility for his actions, it is a rare child indeed that possesses the maturity and experience to do so.

As we have made quite clear, success in America belongs to the individual. Rarely does one look at a highly successful businessman and praise his wife for standing by and supporting her man, putting him through school, raising his children, and nurturing his home all to make it possible for the businessman to be so good at his job. Along the same lines, it is also rare for the wife or parent of a failed businessman to be blamed for his shortcomings in the workplace. His failures at work are typically considered his, and his alone.

Needless to say, America's respect for individuality can negatively impact a child's school behavior and performance. Today, parents are feeling less and less responsible for their child's actions both at home and at school. Children are no longer considered a direct reflection of their parents—not in this day and age of broken homes and increasingly hectic schedules. Gone are the days when parents felt completely responsible for their children's happiness, character, behavior, and school performance. In today's busy world, children fend for themselves while their parents struggle to make ends meet. When a child succeeds in today's society, parents are given little credit; when a child fails, the parents rarely share the blame.

This is not the attitude adopted by most families of Asian descent, ours included. While we embrace American ideals like independence and self-reliance as much as anyone else, we also learned from our parents the importance of shared responsibility. They held themselves primarily responsible for every aspect of our lives, from our character to our education. We are not saying that American parents don't feel responsible for their children—we know they do. What we are saying is that the strong desire for independence that American society fosters in both children and their parents tends to eliminate the need for shared responsibility *earlier* than in families of other cultures. And while this early independence is freeing and satisfying for both parties, it often does little to enhance a child's performance in the classroom.

We learned at an early age that our parents were different. While other parents encouraged their children to get good grades and study hard in order to get good jobs, none were as physically and emotionally invested in their children's academic pursuits as ours were. We have already described how our parents involved themselves in every aspect of our education, from reviewing our textbooks themselves to taking on the role of teacher on a nightly basis, but their intense emotional involvement deserves special mention and praise in this chapter. Our parents firmly believed that they were largely responsible for both our failures and our successes in the classroom, particularly early on in our academic careers. No bad day at the office could affect our father's mood more than a bad grade could—that's how much more important our education and futures were compared to everything else.

Accepting some responsibility for your child's failures in the classroom will stress the value you place on education without stifling your child's independence.

Our parents considered their roles as educators equal or more important to their roles as providers of food, clothing, values, and shelter. Because of their beliefs, we learned quickly that our academic and professional success would determine in large part how successful our parents believed they were. Don't underestimate how passionately children want to make you, as parents, feel a sense of pride in their accomplishments. We now realize how much this desire has contributed to the academic and professional success of many Asian-Americans.

Because our parents felt they were largely responsible for our academic success, they never tired of educating us. When we needed help with a homework assignment or a project, no time was a bad time. Weekends and hours after work were never off limits. In retrospect, we often wonder how our parents always managed to find the time. Our parents never did belittle our questions, no matter how simple or complex, and often spent hours researching the topics that were foreign to them. This was their way of showing they were doing their part to ensure our academic success.

The best way to show your kids that you gladly share responsibility for their education is to be available and enthusiastic when they ask for your help.

Just to show you how important our parents' guidance and constant presence was to our success in school, we again bring up the time our parents and Jane moved to Japan. As you know, when Jane began her freshman year of high school, our parents were working demanding jobs and long hours. Because of their busy schedules, they no longer had the time to spend with Jane and her studies. Quite mistakenly, our parents fooled themselves into believing that at the tender age of fourteen Jane should have already learned the skills to succeed in school without their help.

As you now are aware, our parents were dead wrong. Jane's grades plummeted, and although she was able to turn things around, we all believe with a great deal of certainty that Jane's poor grades during her freshman year prevented her from initially gaining acceptance to the University of North Carolina at Chapel Hill.

And boy did our parents love that UNC. The minute we moved to North Carolina, we recall our parents mentioning how wonderful it was to have such a great state university close by. Throughout North Carolina, UNC was well known for its inexpensive tuition and excellent academic programs. It was also a mere twenty minutes from our house, and after Soo hurriedly left the state for Baltimore, they set their sights on Jane attending their beloved university of choice.

Although Jane ultimately graduated from the University of North Carolina at Chapel Hill with a degree in international relations, most people are unaware that she was initially denied admission. While Jane was disappointed and a little embarrassed (she had always taken for granted that UNC would be among her college options), our parents were devastated. Although they were disappointed with Jane for not putting forth her best effort earlier in high school, they were equally disappointed with themselves for not helping Jane achieve better grades her freshman year. Many of you reading might think this a little absurd—after all, it's Jane's responsibility to study hard and get good grades, right? Well, not according to most Asian parents. Although we can relate to your sentiments, most Asian parents (our parents included) view their children's failures as their own. So, much to Jane's dismay, our parents took the news of her rejection harder than she did.

We'd like to share another example from Jane's life: how our parents accepted responsibility for her failure to pass the bar. Although Jane was in her mid-twenties by the time she graduated from law school and took the bar, our parents still made it a priority to emphasize just how important it was for her to effectively manage her time and study hard during the three months preceding the exam. Even during law school (when the bar was a year or two away), our dad would tell Jane to put forth her best effort in class. According to our dad, law school was simply a means to an end, and the end was passing the bar.

After our family celebrated Jane's graduation, the focus turned to the impending bar exam. Although our parents were hundreds of miles away in North Carolina, they communicated with Jane a couple of times a week via email to provide her with what they referred to as "inspirational pep talks"—what Jane sometimes referred to as "overkill." Today, our family laughs when Jane recalls some of the emails our father had written her. Two of the more memorable emails are pasted below:

To : Jane Kim
From : Jae Kim
Re : How Are You?

Hi Jane. It was a great feeling to see you graduating from Temple and getting a law degree. Mom and I are very proud of you and your accomplishments so far. You must have a suggested study plan for the upcoming bar. The reason I am giving you the hint is that when you are studying based on a daily schedule, you will achieve 30 to 40% better results than those studying without a clear schedule according to a research paper issued by the Harvard Business Review. Think that you are in jail for the next two months for your long-term gain and career. Nelson Mendela spent 26 years in jail, but he studied hard and kept himself in good health. At the end, he became a great president of South Africa. Jane, short-term pain for your long-term gain. You can do it. Please make your own Powerpoint daily schedule in detail (Mon, Tue, Wed, Thu, Fri, Sat, Sun) and send it to me for review. This is very critical for you to succeed and pass the bar exam. I love you. Dad.

Imagine checking your email and seeing this in your inbox! Although it occasionally irritated Jane to receive e-mails such as these, she knew that our parents only wanted the best for her. Yet despite the frequent emails and long hours of studying, Jane did not pass the bar her first time. Although she had spent many hours studying the various subjects, she realized she had not been studying the right way. As she braced herself for a grueling six months ahead (the bar exam is only offered twice a year) our parents felt guilty that they, in part, were responsible for Jane's failure to pass the bar.

While Jane was questioning whether law school was the right career path for her, our parents were blaming themselves for not having spent enough time with their daughter preparing for standardized tests when she was in high school. They understood the importance of building a solid foundation of test preparation skills, and they knew they had put Jane on a less rigorous schedule than Soo. When Jane failed the bar, our parents immediately asked themselves, "What could we have done to prevent this?" Would things have turned out differently if they had spent more time with Jane emphasizing the importance of standardized tests? Should she have taken more practice tests? We'll never know for sure. But with our parents' guidance, Jane changed her study methods, focused 100% of her energies on passing the bar, and was successful the second time around.

Parental involvement need not end after high school; achieving in college and graduate school is perhaps more crucial to professional success in the long term. Keep monitoring your child's success, albeit less rigorously.

In the last chapter we will discuss how this shared responsibility for failures at school can put an exorbitant amount of pressure on children to succeed in school, often with disastrous consequences. We've all heard stories of children who have done the unthinkable (attempted suicide, run away from home) because they were too ashamed to face their parents or feared negative consequences when they failed. Of course, we are not advising parents to put this type of pressure on their children; however, we stand by our belief that accepting at least some responsibility for your children's failures at school will help them academically. Remember, as we discussed in Secret 2, academic successes should be seen as triumphs for the entire family.

We don't want parents to accept responsibility for *all* their children's failures or disappointments; after all, children must eventually and ultimately accept responsibility for their own actions. But it's important to lay the groundwork for an elevated sense of family responsibility. You can't expect a nine-year-old to fully understand that working hard in school is much more beneficial to his long-term success than playing two hours of video games a day. Priorities for children are not inherent; they are learned and taught by their parents. Although Jane was old enough to understand that she needed good grades to get into a top college, she was still too young and undisciplined to study hard without parental supervision. It is up to parents to help their children decide what's most important (and to show continued involvement in their successes and failures). Despite any resistance your child may put up as a youngster, take solace in the knowledge that they'll undoubtedly thank you many years later.

Secret 17: To-Do List

- Accepting some responsibility for your child's failures in the classroom will stress the value you place on education without stifling your child's independence.
- The best way to show your kids that you gladly share responsibility for their education is to be enthusiastic and available when they need your help.
- Parental involvement need not end after high school; college and graduate school achievement is perhaps more crucial to professional success in the long term, and should also be monitored, albeit less rigorously.

Afterword

Where Asian Parents Go Wrong

If you think we have all the answers, think again. Asians may make up a disproportionate percentage of the student population at the top universities, but they are also plagued by the highest suicide rate amongst college students and young adults. We may be doing something right, but we're also doing some things wrong.

In addition to being viewed as obedient and gifted in the classroom, Asians are often seen as rigid and one-dimensional. As sad as it is to say, the very secrets that Asian parents use to raise children who are successful in the classroom can backfire when pursued without the right intentions.

So let's begin discussing where Asian parents go wrong. It all starts with Secret 1—instilling a love and need for learning and education. This is the most important of our secrets, and not surprisingly, the most difficult to practice. It goes without saying, then, that some Asians don't practice this particular secret well. As we have mentioned throughout this book, Asians are men and women of ritual. Because of this, many Asian immigrant parents don't find it difficult to instill the *need* for learning and education in their children. They focus on homework and lessons, drilling concept after concept into their children. What they don't realize, however, is that the *love* for learning and education is more important that the *need*. Time and time again we have seen well accomplished and highly educated Asian-Americans fail to reach their potential because there is no joy in their hearts for acquiring knowledge. They know how to study, assimilate knowledge, and fill their houses with diplomas, but they do not enjoy the process of learning or earning the degrees. These Asian men and women will look at their diplomas hanging on their walls or the suffixes attached to their names with short-lived pride. On the other hand, men and women who love learning will experience the lifetime of joy (and pride!) that knowledge can bring.

Asian parents often fail in this regard because they are consumed by ritual. They enforce a strict and rigid schedule for studies that cannot be altered; they believe in performing mind-numbingly boring exercises again and again until a concept is drilled home. There is little fun interjected into these hours dedicated to academic pursuits, mainly because these parents mistakenly believe that fun and education are separate and distinct entities.

Because of this attitude, some of our Asian friends and colleagues view their childhood as nothing more than an endless series of lectures, homework assignments, and competitions. Asian parents who deprive their children of fun during their formative years by centering all activities around homework or goal-oriented activities are forgetting that Secret 1 involves instilling a passion for learning. This passion is fostered by making learning fun and rewarding—not by forcing it down the throats of children without much-needed periods of rest and relaxation. We know many instances where well meaning but overzealous parents spent all their energy and time instructing their children without *having fun*. Children who view learning and education as a chore due to strict or overbearing parents will never continue the joyful quest for higher education and knowledge once they are away from home. A good rule of thumb is this: if you're not having fun, you're kids aren't either.

There are unfortunately many more examples of Asian parents guilty of depriving their children of a normal and happy childhood than we would care to admit. One particularly sad story comes to mind that involves a Korean-American we will call "Sandy."

Sandy was the only child of two Korean immigrants, who we'll call Mr. and Mrs. Song. Mr. Song was the only son in his family, and hence the only man able to keep his family name alive. Rumor has it that he was severely disappointed when he and his wife were only able to have a daughter.

Whatever bitterness and disappointment Mr. Song felt must have been short-lived, because we never knew a father more devoted to his daughter's education and future. Quite frankly, his devotion bordered on the fanatical. Sandy was ten when the Songs moved to Raleigh and joined our church. We remember her as a cute girl with long eyelashes and a shy smile. We also remember Sandy never being able to join us for birthday or slumber parties, despite numerous invitations from our parents. Sandy's own eleventh birthday party was cut short after only two hours, with Mr. Song constantly watching the clock at Chuck E. Cheese's and rushing everyone out the door before all the children could finish their birthday cake. Later we found out that Mr. Song wanted to make sure his daughter was able to complete the arithmetic exercises he had assigned her for the weekend.

Mr. Song kept his daughter on a tight schedule. The whole family would wake up at 5:30 A.M. and drive to the family business, an Asian grocery store. From six to seven, Sandy would tackle advanced arithmetic problems handpicked by her father. At the dot of seven, Mr. Song would drive his daughter to school. After school was over, he would pick his daughter up and drive back to the store. Sandy would then complete her homework with the help of her parents. After closing the store, returning home, and eating dinner, Sandy and her father would continue to work on an advanced curriculum of mathematics and science for hours.

Sandy was a gifted girl with a knack for mathematics. To the pleasure of her father, she excelled in this area at school and was soon taking classes with students many years older than she. Mr. Song continued his frantic pace of study with his daughter throughout middle school and high school, and at last his efforts were rewarded. Sandy was awarded a full scholarship to an Ivy League university.

Unfortunately, this story doesn't have a happy ending. Although Sandy had excelled academically, she had never experienced the fun-filled birthday parties, vacations, dates, or proms that make up the childhood memories of most men and women. Because her father had stressed study and work over fun for most of her life, Sandy never developed the love for learning and higher education that some other students did. When she went off to college, where her father could no longer directly supervise her every move, you can guess what happened. Finally free to do what she wanted and to experience the fun she had been missing, Sandy stopped studying and began partying it up. She hung out with the wrong crowd and even dabbled in drugs. Two years later, she lost her scholarship after failing to maintain a 3.0 grade point average. Although she was able to graduate from college, Sandy became a disillusioned young adult who never associated learning and higher education with joy or personal fulfillment. She never reached her full potential, and the last we heard, she and her father were barely speaking to one another.

Depriving your child of a normal and happy childhood because of overly ambitious academic goals can have disastrous consequences. Remember that in order for your child to view learning as fun and rewarding, you must *make* learning fun and rewarding for him or her. That involves providing your child with plenty of happy memories involving activities that are both academically and nonacademically based. A true love for learning will ensure that your child will be committed to higher education long after you are gone.

Another skill that some Asian parents fail to import to their kids is the ability to speak different languages. One of the most important things you can pass onto your children is the gift of gab. If you are a parent who speaks another language, it is crucial that you pass this asset onto your children. While most adults take several years or a lifetime to master a foreign language, children learn things at lightning speed and can easily pick up two or three different tongues without difficulty. Some parents have expressed reservation about teaching their children a second or third language, for fear of overwhelming them. Our advice is this: They won't be over whelmed; rather, they'll be thankful years later.

You might be surprised to know that our own parents didn't teach us to speak Korean when we were young. When we asked them why, they regretfully told us that they feared that teaching us both Korean and English at the same time would confuse us. Although they tried to teach us Korean years later (after we mastered English) by enrolling us in weekend Korean language classes, we never came close to reaching the ultimate goal our parents so desired: to speak fluent Korean.

Today, we live in an increasingly globalized world. As a result of tourism and increased trade with other nations, our world is getting smaller. Having the ability to speak another language will give your child a competitive advantage over his or her peers.

Having the ability to speak another language not only looks good on a resume, but also provides your children with a broadened view of the world. Although this is by no means a scientific fact, we have made one rather interesting discovery: all of our friends and colleagues who speak more than one language tend to more willingly embrace people and ideas from other cultures. They are more eager to learn new things and to keep an open mind. In today's multicultural society, these traits are vital to personal and professional success.

The best example we can share with you is the international high school Jane attended in Tokyo, Japan. At the time, students from forty-two nationalities were represented at her school. Roughly a third spoke a language other than English fluently, and a good portion of the remaining two-thirds could at least hold a conversation in a second language. Many of the cliques and racial tensions that were prevalent in so many American high schools were practically nonexistent at The American School in Japan. Students seemed to accept and embrace other students' differences, while expressing a genuine interest to learn about other cultures and ways of thinking. If they didn't feel this way when they first arrived in Japan, they definitely did when they left (yet another reason to surround your children with similarly minded individuals).

But, what if you can't speak another language? Should you focus on other things to teach your children, such as your hidden talent of belly dancing? Well, maybe. But don't give up just yet! Just because you or your partner is limited to one language does not mean your child is destined to travel down the same path. These days, language schools are a dime a dozen, particularly in metropolitan areas, or areas where various ethnic groups live side by side. For example, in New York City, you can find a language school for almost any language imaginable. Companies are more than aware of the allure of being bilingual or multilingual, and if you can afford it, we believe this skill is worth every penny of your investment.

If you can't afford the cost, there are creative ways to teach your children a second language. Do you have a friend or neighbor who speaks another language? Ask them if they would be willing to tutor your child in their native tongue in exchange for that family recipe of yours they've been pining after for the last year. In addition, high school students are always looking to make some extra cash, so weekly tutoring sessions would work out nicely for both parties. You could even post a job ad at various universities requesting a language tutor—just be sure to ask for references. Finally, many cities and/or communities also have nonprofit organizations whose mission is to advance the causes of various ethnic groups. Talk to the executive director or ask if he or she knows of any nonprofit organizations or individuals that would help your child become bilingual. You might be surprised with the results of your search.

If you're lucky enough to live in California or a smattering of other states that have adopted a foreign language curriculum, your tax dollars are already being put to good use. In 2001, the California State Board of Education adopted a foreign language framework into their public schools for kindergarten to grade 12. This demonstrates that state governments are now openly recognizing the benefits that second-language skills bestow upon students.

When it comes to schoolwork, Asian parents are notorious for putting an enormous amount of pressure on their children. What's worse, they often don't recognize when they do! When we asked our parents' friends and colleagues whether they pressured their children to excel in school, we were surprised at what they said. Approximately a third of them said they never put any pressure on their children, but simply encouraged them to work hard and try their best. Another third said they put pressure on their children only when they knew they weren't trying their best or not reaching their full potential. The remaining third admitted they put some pressure on their children, but raised an interesting question: if they couldn't do it, whose responsibility was it to motivate their kids? After speaking with the parents, we then spent some time with the kids (all adults now) asking them if they felt pressure growing up to excel academically. Regardless of what their parents had said, an overwhelming majority said they felt more than an average amount of pressure. And, the children of the parents who claimed to have never pressured their children were the ones who felt the most pressure!

So . . . what does this tell us? That these parents are delusional? Well, not exactly (although some of the children might think so!). What it does tell us, loud and clear, is that many parents fail to realize just how much pressure they are actually putting on their children. Day after day, year after year, parents *think* they are hands-off and easygoing, while their children are silently buckling under the strain of trying to perform.

Many Asian parents are what we call "results oriented." This means that they place more emphasis on the end result than the means to the end. They often fall into the trap of demanding improvement (or threatening punishment for a lack thereof) without offering any emotional support or strategy to bring it about. As a result, the child of such parents ends up feeling alienated from his or her family. It is important to remember that as a family, you are a team working toward the same goal: academic and professional success for your child. Demanding or telling your child to improve in school without offering the necessary support and guidance will surely backfire.

We'd like to share a story that illustrates this point. Mimi was an outgoing and funny Japanese-American teenager. She was the youngest of three daughters, and although Mimi was an above-average student, she paled in comparison to her sisters. Both Mimi's sisters had been awarded scholarships at top universities; one was studying to be an architect, and the other was a corporate attorney. As long as Mimi could remember, it was expected that she would graduate from an Ivy League university and pursue a high-powered career—just like her siblings. When she was in the ninth grade, Mimi brought home her worst report card ever. Her parents were shocked, never having seen a report card smattered with C's. Their shock, however, soon turned to disappointment and anger. Mimi remembers being lectured for over an hour by her parents about how disappointed they were, how she would not be able to get into a respectable college, and that she should have learned how to study from her two older sisters. She remembers barely saying a word, and when the lecture was over, she was no better off than she was before. However, her parents did make one thing crystal clear: improve your grades, or you will be grounded indefinitely. Although her parents didn't say it, Mimi also got another message that day: improve your grades or be considered a failure who brings shame to your family.

After the talk, Mimi felt like a complete failure. At that moment, she believed the only thing she could do to please her family would be to get good grades. She vowed she would never let her parents down again and set out to earn their love again (or so she believed) by getting good grades on her report card. For most of the next quarter, Mimi studied like a fiend. She quit the softball team and took a leave of absence from the school newspaper. All her free time during school was spent in the library, and since she was not allowed to see her friends outside of school, she felt even more alienated and alone.

Things got worse after Mimi received her next report card. Although she had improved quite a bit, she had gotten a C+ in both physics and English literature. In her short life, Mimi recalls never feeling more alone. By not getting a report card with mostly A's, she felt as if she had betrayed her parents. She also told us she started to believe she might be stupid after all. The entire bus ride home, Mimi thought about how she would break the news to her parents and how they would react to her report card. She decided that her parents would be so disappointed in her, she couldn't bear it. That's when she came up with a plan to "change" the two grades on her report card. When she got home, Mimi copied and pasted a B+ over both her physics and English literature grades. The next day at school she Xeroxed a copy of the revised report card and handed the new and improved version to her parents.

Mimi's parents were thrilled—and for the time being, Mimi's secret was safe. Because they were so happy with her improvement at school, they showered her with gifts, praise, had and something she lacked all quarter: freedom to live a normal life again. But as we all know from past experiences, lying is *never* a good solution. The next quarter, Mimi once again struggled with physics and English lit, and her geometry grade also fell. She had hoped her grades would improve so she wouldn't have to deceive her parents again, making the fake report card a one-time offense. But Mimi had now dug herself into a hole, and she convinced herself it would be easier to lie again than to face her parents' anger. And so the cycle continued.

Mimi continued doing this for three quarters until her parents discovered what was going on. When her parents' initial anger had worn off, they asked her why she would resort to such extreme measures to cover up her grades. Her parents explained they were most disappointed in the fact that she had lied, and felt betrayed as a result of the deceit—not the grades. They told her all she needed to do was ask them for help and they would have either helped her themselves, or helped her implement a strategy to improve. Mimi was shocked. She felt compelled to lie about her grades because of the way her parents reacted the first time she slipped. She had never heard her parents communicate their willingness to help before.

So, what's the moral of this story? If we were to pick one, it would be that communication with your child is key. If you fail to ask your child how he is feeling and what you can do to help him improve his grades, then you are not communicating effectively. If you are angry, be sure to cool down and collect your thoughts before speaking with him. You don't want to say anything you will regret later. Furthermore, be sure to make it clear that you are not disappointed in him *as your child*, but rather, you are disappointed with his *grades*. Help your children develop a strategy or plan for their success, and communicate to them that you believe in them. Open and honest communication will help diffuse some of the pressure your children face.

As you can see, Asian parents do not have all the answers. But we feel that as a whole, they're doing something right. Throughout this book, we have recommended strategies to help your child excel in the classroom and experience the joy that comes with intellectual fulfillment and academic achievement. Now that we have come to the end of our journey, we want to review some of our secrets, as well as touch upon our most prized secret to academic success: discipline.

If you ask most Americans (or most anyone in the world) what they believe the key to Asian success in the classroom is, the overwhelming majority would say discipline. According to their peers, Asians are a disciplined people; in other words, they are able to exercise a considerable amount of self-control. Right now you may be wondering why "instilling discipline" was not one of the secrets included in our book; after all, discipline is a frequent subject in most parenting and family magazines in addition to parenting books. Our answer to you is that our *entire book* is centered on instilling discipline in your child. For example, instilling a love of learning and education, getting your child to embrace being a student, teaching your child to delay gratification and embrace sacrifice, setting short- and long-term educational goals—all of those secrets both build and require discipline.

Like most things, there is no one way to gain the discipline and self-control needed to embrace the years of schooling that we believe lead to academic and professional success—but we believe our seventeen secrets will help. We strongly believe that disciplined parents are more likely to raise disciplined children. In other words, you as a parent are your child's most valuable role model.

In summary, Asian students excel in the classroom because we are *raised* to succeed academically. Early in our childhood, our parents instilled in us a love for learning and education, the ability to delay gratification and embrace sacrifice, as well as a fierce sense of family pride and loyalty that would serve us well in the classroom for years to come. While we were attending school, our parents further impressed upon us the importance of competition, setting and achieving both short- and long-term goals, surrounding ourselves with like-minded friends, and regarding our educators with only the utmost respect. Our parents were actively involved in all aspects of our education, and they ensured their daughters would be grateful for all the opportunities America afforded them—in particular, the joy that comes from intellectually challenging, prestigious, and financially rewarding professions. Our hope to all of our readers is that your kids will be as happy in their careers as we are now . . . and as grateful to you as we are to our parents!